The Hardened Years of

Dr. Joseph C. Calkowski

THE HARDENED YEARS OF

Dr. Joseph C. Calkowski

DOCTOR OF ARCHAEOLOGY

JOSEPH CALKOWSKI

THE HARDENED YEARS OF DR. JOSEPH C. CALKOWSKI DOCTOR OF ARCHAEOLOGY

iUniverse books may be ordered through booksellers or by contacting:

iUniverse
1663 Liberty Drive
Bloomington, IN 47403
www.iuniverse.com
1-800-Authors (1-800-288-4677)

ISBN: 978-1-5320-3036-9 (sc)
ISBN: 978-1-5320-3035-2 (e)

Library of Congress Control Number: 2017914255

Print information available on the last page.

iUniverse rev. date: 09/18/2017

I REMEMBER LIKE IT WAS YESTERDAY. There was good old Canyon Blvd. and my house in Madison, Ca. It was the fall of 1982. Summer had ended and school was just beginning, and there was my younger brother and I in our stupid hoods. That didn't matter because my siblings and I were all excited for school. I know, what child or teenager gets excited for school, but we were. Oh, how badly we were mostly because we were each entering a new world in our life, a new beginning, and a new era of school.

Some fathers were Baptist, and some fathers were Christians. Our father was a Plymouth man. He liked to watch every single cent, and he would always find himself in his Plymouth like he was in the Indy 500.

Victoria and Henry would find that watching us was hilarious because right after breakfast they would watch our mother preparing us for school. And that was just like wrestling.

By the time that we were ready, Greg and I would look like two bundled up kids ready for the rain even though there would be no rain outside. Our mother stuffed our faces and our bodies into hoods. You could barely see our faces. Sometimes my mom was about to give me my medication but ended up almost giving it to Greg because you could only see our noses and mouths.

Our older brother and our sister would laugh at us and call us "pimples" because we were such a pain to deal with. Then once we were wrapped our mom would have to take everything off to tell which one was which.

Our father would be outside honking and revving that Plymouth with black exhaust coming from the tail pipe. Our Hillbilly's, neighbor's father, would find it dangerous just to park in back of our father's old

Plymouth. It didn't matter how far back they parked their cars because they would still end up filthy with our father's black exhaust. Then our father would be honking and yelling saying, "come on you little sons of bitches." And before this though, our older brother and our older sister would be gone with the wind because they did not want to deal with the embarrassment.

While our mother tried to see us off, that Plymouth would break down and come rolling back about five times into our driveway. Then he'd have to rev it up again because the engine would turn so cold overnight. Then our father would not be only cursing at us in his crappy Plymouth, but he would be cursing at his Plymouth too saying things like, "Come on you hot damn no good son of a bitch" when he only wishes the engine was warm.

Halfway down the street, after he would finally get the Plymouth out, the Plymouth would break down all over again. And then he would have to start revving it up again with the black exhaust all the way up Canyon Blvd. We would try and waive to our mother from the back window, but could not even see our own mama because he would leave a cloud of black smoke that thick.

My younger brother Greg and I were very excited for our older brother Henry and our beautiful sister. You see my beautiful sister, Victoria, was headed back to high school and this time she was taking Henry with her. Henry was very excited to enter high school, and my sister was very excited to be nominated for queen of many high schools.

The city was choosing the most beautiful girls out of the high schools in my city. My sister was nominated to become queen so it was a very big honor for her. My sister was so excited.

However, Jessie a princess, had a father who worked for the city and she was very jealous of Victoria becoming queen because she felt she was more beautiful than my sister. Jessie went to her father and said, "Daddy, daddy, I want to be the queen of my city." Girls at the high school and people in the city said, "I'm not beautiful enough to be chosen queen and that Victoria Sudomir is."

I should be queen of the city because I am more beautiful than her daddy. You work for the city, daddy, so help make me be the queen and get Victoria out of that royal seat. Jessie, the one with that big ego, begged and cried to her daddy that she wanted her father to do this. Her father tried to explain that he couldn't possibly try to do this to Victoria. It would look bad on him in the City Hall because it would seem like favoritism. And do you think it would look good for you at school?

All the princess' would hate you and the word would go around high school saying that you stole the seat. Can't you just wait one more year to become queen? And she said, "No, I want to be queen now." He said, "Okay, but let's just see what happens. And if things are said about this at the high school you do not blame me.

Her father went to the city and spoke to the Royal Court and explained his situation. And so they said, "You have to explain to Victoria that it is not considered favoritism. That it is his daughter's doing. He said, "We all still believe that you are more beautiful enough to be queen. I even believe that you deserve the honor to be queen. But what can I say, Victoria, my daughter is crying and begging and pleading. She won't let up. So I hope you understand my situation."

When my sister came home that day, she was furious that this happened and said, "What a snake. What an egotistical bitch." When the crown was put on the queen in front of the princess', they already knew that she had to go to daddy to get it because it was all over high school already. They knew that Jessie stole Victoria's crown. The princess' told every single girl in high school.

She tried going to daddy again to see if any of the princess' could be expelled from school including Victoria, but her father said, "I almost lost my job doing this for you. And I told you if you do this, what would be the consequences. So you will have to deal with it."

The day of the Christmas parade, Jessie had to waive her hand and smile and cry to the crowd. She cried because of happiness or because she knew that she was second best and had to go to daddy to get that crown. She even put my sister down a little bit from her probably because she knew that my sister would stand out more beautiful than she.

Victoria's eyes were open for the first time on how deception can happen amongst girls in the Royal Court. There was one consequence that her father did not tell her daughter. It was that, if his daughter was made queen of our city in 1982, she could never again be chosen to be in the Royal Court. And Victoria would have as many chances to be queen as long as the Royal Court existed.

Unfortunately, Victoria graduated in "83 and was not nominated queen. That Christmas the whole family knew that we had to make our sister feel real special and loved. So there were many hugs and kisses for Victoria and telling her she's the most beautiful sister in the world.

Tata is how we would say dad in Polish. Tata bought the most beautiful Christmas tree that year to make Victoria and the whole family feel better and to show just how much he loved everyone in the household.

I believe Victoria was very happy with Tata for what he had done and how her brothers felt about her. She felt very special that she was the queen of our whole family that year. Tata even let her put the head ornament on the Christmas tree, the angel. She almost fell off the ladder while walking up the ladder. But Greg and I, with our buck teeth, said, "Don't worry, Victoria, We'll hold the ladder for you."

Now Henry, my older brother, had just begun high school that fall. My brother was a musician in junior high. He had played the violin in an orchestra. One of the best songs I heard play was the Star Wars Theme, and I was very proud of him back then. In high school they had no orchestra so he changed to the guitar and keyboard, and he was looking to be picked by a band. It wasn't very long before he was chosen to be in the band called London after Midnight. He kept his head held high and never gave up hope.

In fall of '82, Greg and I entered elementary school. And boy our eyes were really open to racism. We already had racism going on from our Hillbilly neighbors almost every single day. Our Hillbilly neighbor's father would always try to fight my father who was an older man. You see my father married our mother when she was 28 and he was 62.

They had Henry the next year and me when my father was 69. T They had my younger brother Greg when my father was 71 going on 72. But I guess I'm going too far back into the past. Like I said, my siblings and I had our eyes opened to racism.

Our Hillbilly, neighbor's kids were becoming skinheads and my younger brother and I, while in elementary school every day, saw my younger brother in the kindergarten play area to keep an eye on him.

I had to deal with a lot of white supremacy. I made a best friend in the meantime. His name was Jaden Gordon who was a young black kid. When they picked on him, I would always watch his back because not only was he my best friend, but we became blood-brothers that year by cutting each other's fingertips, holding each other's hands, and said blood-brothers for life.

When they tried to pick on him they wanted to hurt him physically all because he was black. Now my neighbor's kid helped get a lot of that white supremacy going. When I told Jaden to step aside so I could handle it, they thought that I was nothing more than a dumb Pollock. They told me to step aside but I said, "What are you doing to my brother?" They did not understand the colored kid that they were about to beat up was not only my best friend but my blood-brother.

I said, "If you don't want trouble you sure picked the wrong kid to hurt. I said, "You are going to have me all over you now." Luckily my old man taught me a thing or two of how to take care of punks like those. Guys like those made me have seizures during the daytime and made me cry due to a lot of stress and anger. They made fun of me by pretending they were convulsing and having a seizures.

I was having seizures every single day. My seizures were lasting by the minutes. Ambulance bills were hitting my father hard.

My father was once so angry that he asked me if I knew where those punk kids lived so he could give those bills to their parents. One time, though, he got so angry because I couldn't find out where those kids lived and all the bills came onto him over and over. He had to make payment plans in order to take care of them. After that he became so angry, and he gave me a good lashing because of all the bills and because of me having seizures due to me listening to the kids.

My mother was on the other side of the coin now. If my dad didn't give me money, my mother would. My mother would take Greg and I to Kmart and all three of us would have a great time. But soon Greg and I would be away from our mother, and we would end up lost. Then Greg would start crying and so I would take him to the service desk and have our mother paged. Everyone would here the page and the store reprensentative would say, "Mrs. Calkowski, your two little boys are at the service desk."

After shopping, our mother would call our father for a ride home. On the way home, our mother would tell our father how bad we were crying because we got lost. Then my father would reply and say to us, "Do I have a bunch of cry-babies for sons?" And all the time in KMART, if we wanted a toy or something, and our mother said we couldn't have it, we would scream and cry.

We also gave our sister a lot of worries too even though we loved our sister. I recall one time our sister was taking us up to see her friend who lived in the foothills of our city. It was about the same time that I was about seven and Greg was about five and we went in her crappy green Plymouth. But just like any kid, we always had to touch something when our elders told us not to.

Anyway, Victoria was at her friend's house and was wondering what the brake cord in the middle of the seat was. Then Greg and I started messing around with it. But then we had unlocked the brakes and we started rolling backwards downhill. And then Victoria's friend asked, isn't that your Plymouth going downhill?" Victoria explained that her little brothers were in the Plymouth so they went running after them down the street.

We tried to step on the accelerator, but we didn't know the accelerator from the brake. And anytime we stepped on the accelerator, it would make a crackling noise. I could only step on the accelerator since that was all I could reach. We had tried to lift up what we had shut down. It turned out to be the break release.

We did not know, "like idiots", that we had to press the button again and pull it up to stop us from moving. All she could see us doing was crying like babies. And all we could think of was that we were going to die. However, that's what kids get who get too curious and love to press buttons. Luckily, our sister's pinto crashed into a bush.

Our sister, Victoria and her friend, got us out and we were doing nothing but panting crying. We were saying, "Victoria, we didn't mean to do it." It was just like any kid who does not want to get themselves into trouble and admit it. She started hugging and kissing us because she was relieved we were okay and she was the one babysitting us. Victoria even had some nicknames for us. My nickname was "Mooses" and Greg's nicknames was "Cooses". Crazy nicknames though, huh.

Our parents eventually found out what had happened that night and so we had to step up and tell what we did, especially, since our sister had her thumb and index finger around each other's ears. You see, she knew that she would not get paid her allowance because of what happened. Luckily, the person whose bush we crashed into did not prosecute. He was more concerned about us being alive still.

Our sister loved to tease us so at times. Well you know how some women put cold cream all over their faces, our sister would put some sort of green cold cream all over her face at night. She would scare us just after she had put that stuff on and came out of the bathroom. She would find us hiding from her when she came out of the bathroom because of that cold cream all of her face. She would also come after us with those creepy nails and waive them at us and call out our names.

Sometimes our sister would also chase us with that white Noxzema all over her face until we were crying. We would be crying and screaming for our mama. Our mama would say, "Oh my God in Polish; what are you doing?" Our father would be laughing his ass off along with my brother.

Our mama was very angry and asked her to say she was sorry but we were too scared at the time because she stilled had that cold cream on her face. So when she turned around to say that she was sorry, Greg and I would just run out the door in tears. Our mother would say to her, "Must you wear that stuff on your face?" And father would get into a little argument that would lead to a big one all because of a difference of opinion. Their fights were always that way, a difference of opinion.

You see on my block there were some couples that would just laugh about their arguments, and some of them beat their significant others. Then they would go out for a smoke or a drink. And in my eyes, my parents raising hell all because a difference of an opinion was a very stupid thing to do.

It wasn't long before some years went by, and I started to try and take on the world by myself. I would be watching and protecting my brother from our father. My father always told me to let things blow over your shoulder, but it was hard to listen to him when you're a kid at seven years old. I found myself causing the trouble in my family.

It wasn't long before some years went by, and I started to try and take on the world by myself. I would be watching and protecting my brother from our father. My father always told me to let things blow over your shoulder, but it was hard to listen to him when you're a kid at seven years old. I found myself causing the trouble in my family.

And because I caused a lot of trouble in the family with the bills, my mother and father would constantly yell at each other. And those stressful arguments would cause me to get seizures. I became a rebel then. I went out into the streets to fight for gratification. I became known as great street fighter.

And so everyone wanted to prove themselves as a street fighter because to fight me was to fight a real street fight. Guys would try to not only hurt my blood brother Jaden, but my brother too. They knew family and friends would draw me out, but I learned from my old man to just walk away.

I learned a lot from my old man, and he had taught me well. Some of those things that he had taught me, I did not use though. I was just supposed to take it. But just like every other kid, I had to learn things the hard way in life. And then all of the street fighters wanted to fight me just to fight me. Soon all our neighbors were fighting each other, and brothers were fighting brothers; some brothers fought other neighbors who were older just to see how tough they were.

THE BLAME GAME AND
THE CONSEQUENCES

I N OUR NEIGHBORHOOD, PEOPLE WOULD like to take on some of the two best fighters like our best friends who were twins. Their names were Brian and Bruce. Oh boy! Did they fight for fun. And they did not only fight each other but Sam and Jack too. Oh then it became a fight with Manny and Sam. And man now it became about money. Some guys took bets to see just how bloody it would get and who would actually win. They had become one of the best fighters on the block, and I had lost some fights to them.

I also had become one of the best Q ball players in town. And to play me you had to be prepared to lose some money or else gain a busted lip, black eye, or a busted nose! I had made a name for myself on streets, or should I say, guys had nicknamed me. I had to watch-out also the ASP because I had to be just as wicked as one those boys. I should have never took those names because .those names are the kind of names you have to live up to. You know you would have to put up a front if you did not have the money. But one time in grade school, I was about to go up against one of the hardest challenges of my life.

My teacher wanted to know what had happened to my hand, and I had blamed my old man becuase we had an argument the night before. And boy, did I see a chance to get back at him. I took it without thinking first of what might happen to me or my father. I was put in foster care, and children services got involved with my family and I. I had never been so scared for myself and as well as my father.

I also had almost drowned while in that foster care home and luckily,

1

I was okay. Nobody was watching me around the pool when anything can happen. It was reported to children services. It was all because of what I had done just to get revenge over a stupid argument I had with my father. So to any children, teenager, or young adult that may be reading this book, I'd like to say, "Treasure your parents because you'll never know when you may actually want them beside you that bad."

When I was in that foster home, I cried every night for my father just to be able to touch his hand or just to give him a kiss on the cheek or even a hug. It would have meant the world to me. There was a court date though to go to. My father fought just to get his son back. And So I fessed up in front of that judge and told the truth about it just being a lie. I was just angry with my father.

The judge asked me why did I lie? I explained to the judge that I was just angry at my father from the night before, and that I would never do this again if you give custody back to my father. The judge disagreed and gave custody to my mother on one condition: that children servies could stop in and speak to my family and myself to see how the family is doing as well as myself.

It was like having a piece of my father's heart torn out, and I felt like I was losing my father all over again. And, oh boy, did I cry in that courtroom that day because they wanted to arrest my father. It would have been all because of me.

One time when social services came to our home, a woman named Mrs. Smith insulted my old man. She said to him, "He was not a good father." My father then replied in his own home, "You're saying I am not a good father? I raised four children and one of them was from my wife's first marriage. I raised her as my own daughter and brought up three boys. I've given them shelter, food, and love. And you dare tell me that I am not a good father."

That got my father so angry that he said to this woman, "You get your things, your stupid counseling and criticism, and get the hell out of my home. You go and rattle someone else's cage you old battle-axe witch." Mrs. Smith then said, "I had never been so insulted in my entire life.' My father then said, "He was honored to be the first." My whole family laughed so hard that night and gave my father hugs and kisses.

On the streets, not only did I get into fights, but I got into trouble with the police. And because of the the nicknames that I had to try and live up to. A couple of times my father tried to teach me that sometimes you just cannot have fast food and you have to eat what's at home. I ended up calling the police on him. My father had gotten me so angry by saying, "We have bread, we have eggs, we have water, milk, and we have butter so you don't need any money to go out."

Around this time in my life, I was around nine or ten, and I thought I could get away with anything. So I would call the police and say that my father was starving me. And when they came, they laughed in my face. The police said, "Your father's not starving you, Joseph. You have a whole fridge full of food." My father would tell them, "That's what I've been trying to tell him, Officer."

The police would then explain to me, "You know, Joseph, there are some people out there in the city that don't have one penny to get anything to eat. Remind yourself that, Joseph. They said because now you're acting like a spoiled little brat that we have to deal with every single day.' My father said, "Is there any way officers' that you can put a leash on my son?" And the police just laughed.

We basically were spoiled because our mother brought us up spoiled. And so we took advantage. But our father, he would never allow it. If we tried to scream, our father would bust us in our chops; or if we did something bad, he would bring out the board or the belt. Mostly it was my younger brother who did a lot of bad things.

Now since my younger brother and I were both skinny, one of us would have to take a beating. So I hid my little brother, Greg in the closet, and my father knew that it was Greg who had done whatever he did. Then I told my father, "No I did it." And even though my father knew that I did not do it, I knew that I needed to convince him so I would break something or do something wrong right in front of him.

Then he would say, "Okay I believe you now, you little son of a bitch." And I would take the board or the belt. Luckily, even though I was skinny, I had a hard rear. You see, even though I was the middle one, I was the strongest amongst Henry and Greg. I could take anything. I could take punches, lashings, and beatings from the board, etc.

Even emotionally, I could take things stronger than my brothers. Boy my younger brother Greg and I had some duzzies together fighting growing up. We made a mean pair too. I tried to show him how to throw mean punches, so if I were not around, he could fend for himself.

We hung out with Brian, Manny, Sam, and Jack, and boy, all of them loved to piss off our father by egg throwing and name calling. And since they would love doing it my father, he would try and not let them get away. He would even chase after our best friends Brian and Manny.

Their grandmother even looked after Greg and myself when we were younger and growing up with them playing marbles, collecting hot wheels, and kid stuff, but once out that door, we were all on our own.

THROUGH THE 80'S LOOKING GLASS BUT INTO THE 90'S

I N THE FIFTH GRADE, THE public school said we cannot have a boy with seizures on our grounds. Luckily, my mother's friend found a school in another city called A private school for the physically and Orthopedically Handicapped Children.

I attended a private school from the fifth grade until I had to go to high school. While in that private school, I was treated equally amongst the rest of the students. I made a lot of friends and there have been friends I lost contact with but will never forget. Some of them I do see, though very rare. There was a hand bell choir that I was in while attending A private school. Everyone in the choir had a friend named Anthony Romero. He was everyone's friend. Anthony was unlike any of us. He was in a wheel chair because he had jaw lock and braces on his arms. It made his arms hard to move and his speech was hard to understand, but being his friend, we got to know how to speak to Anthony and understand him very well.

Before he used to just watch us play from the background of the room where we practiced. Then one day Anthony came in with one of those little keyboards playing many little tunes. He played Christmas tunes and all kinds of songs that we hardly knew how to play. He moved his arms side to side with the braces on and then tapped the keys on the keyboard.

Our bell choir director was very moved as we all were. So he joined our hand bell choir, and through The Make-A-Wish Foundation, he was given a huge keyboard so he could join our choir and be a part of our group. He was a great friend, but because he went to a different high school, I could never see him again. Maybe one day I could see if fate has a hand, but until then, he will always be in my mind and in my heart.

I was thirteen going on fourteen when I started high school. The 80s' was an interesting era for all of us. So many things happened that we would never forget. The "Rock N Roll" music of the 80s' was fantastic.

There was a former actor who had become president, and I'd say, "A damn good president." His name was Ronald Regan. He made communism fall by having stood up to this German communist aggressor named Garbageov tear down the wall of communism. Our President Raegan, God Rest His Soul in Peace, went over into Germany and said to Garbageov as he was standing on the wall "You tear down this wall." And so the wall of communism was torn down.

It was a highlighted moment in American World History. Europe is now a peaceful and free country due to our president's actions. Bruce Jackson had made some great albums such as: Thriller and Beat It and also Billy Jean and the Dog Gone Girl is mine. As you can see, the 80s' was just great. The 80s', if I could describe it in any way would be, "sex, love, and rock and roll"!!!!!

I did not do so well my freshman year the first time around. But the second time around, I completed it. A lot of the guys from the streets still called me, "Watch-out," or "The ASP." But since I started bragging about my royal blood, they started making fun of me.

I found that a lot of jocks were beating their girlfriends. I tried to tell the campus guards about what was happening and all they had to say was, "If she wants to get beat, Joseph, let her get beat. It's not our problem." I told them you're responsible for student safety. Every student on these grounds is your problem. All they would say is, "Just leave it alone, Joseph."

However, I did not leave it alone. I went to confront the jock and would kick that jock's ass. Their girlfriend, however, would give me the most stupid question you could possibly imagine. Why did you do that, Joseph? I replied, "Excuse me, your boyfriend smacked you, called you a bitch, or sometimes they would call them a whore or slut. Then demand a kiss from them." And then I would say, and you're asking me, why I did that.

Then they would give me the most stupid answer you could possibly think of. But I love him. I got kicked out from many high schools for the same reason. In all those high schools, they all gave me the same stupid question and the same stupid answer.

When I was fourteen though, there was a city talent show to which I had entered. My father sat in the first row. I won first place right in front of my father. My father got up and said, "That's my boy." He was never really more proud of me, and I was glad that I had made him proud that year.

On October 8th, 1991, which was the next year, my father had died. I was fifteen and Greg was twelve. Our father was eighty-five at the time of his death. Something very ironic happened though. Exactly one week before my father's death, his nephew died of aneurism in the brain, and my father died a week later. Exactly seven days of aneurism in the stomach. Luckily before my father's death, Victoria had gotten married to a man named Murray, and Victoria was blessed to have my father give her away.

My mom and dad danced as lovers on Victoria's wedding day. They were so happy for Victoria. It was too bad our dad was not around for her daughter, Annmarie, being born two years later in May of '93. Damn, he would have been so happy to be a grandfather to her child.

My sister was just as upset with my father's death because her own father was never there for her. My father raised her as his own since she was two years old. Her children today though consider my father still to be their real grandfather even though Victoria's true father is still alive.

It's not just because he had raised her, but because, Victoria tried to tell her own father that he was a grandfather and, he didn't respond well. It was because Victoria spoke very little polish now so he denied Victoria as his daughter and said, "Since I don't have no daughter, I do not have any grandchildren."

One thing I will always regret is that I was in the hospital at the time of my father's death. I was getting some counseling but something happened very ironically in the hospital. Also my family came to tell me that my father had died, but that morning I had had a dream that my father was saying goodbye to me, and I woke up hyperventilating.

My sister told a nurse not to tell me one single thing, and the nurse kept her word. All she did was wake me up and told me that my family was here. But when I saw the looks on their faces, I already knew from the dream that I had that my father was gone. My family thought though that the nurse had told me already. But when I told them about my dream, they could not believe that my father came to me in a dream and said goodbye to me.

In the meantime, I had been working on a sunburst drawing for my father. It was just in time for the funeral. Ironically, it had all my father's favorite colors. I did not notice that until the day of the funeral. So I rolled up the sunburst drawing and put it unerneathe my father's arm. Then I kissed him on the forehead to say goodbye.

I had never been in more tears in my entire life. I remained in exile for two years. My mother begged me to start drawing sunbursts again and to start making art period, but I just couldn't bring myself to do this in my exile. Though I tried to continue, I couldn't because my work would either come out too bright or too dark. My days of being an artist I knew were now over.

So now my last greatest piece of artwork is six feet under in my father's casket. My father's reading of the will had come and it seems as though our father had left a small fortune to all of his four boys. Oh, I forgot to mention, I also had a half-brother. His name was Joshua. I also had a half-sister from my father. The same father but different mother. Their mother was dead. She died of polio when it was very big back in the day just like aids is today.

My half-sister killed herself just before I was born. She ate a bullet because of problems with her ex-husband and that's why they got divorced. Anyhow, like I was talking about before, there was a small fortune that my father had left his four boys and nothing was left to our mother. My father usually had a reason for everything he did in life just like how he chose stocks in the stock market. So I just wanted to leave what my father did not leave to my mother in his will well enough alone.

I did not know I was going to be pushed into what may have been one of the hardest choices in my life. I actually had to decide whether or not I could fight my mother in court.

You see my mom was a woman who was promised financial well-being by my father for the rest of her life. So by my father not leaving my mother anything was against his word. And to my mother's family, it was a big no-no. I was thinking that if my mom got homestead like she was fighting for she may kick us all out of the house. That's why I decided to go with my brother Joshua.

Joshua now really hated my mother at the time but was just like I did that our mother may kick us our. However, Victoria said, "That as long as my mother's alive, no one can touch the house." I found out all that Joshua wanted was the house sold to get his money. I then changed sides and sided with my mother and older brother Henry Jr. My mom then got her homestead approved.

People from social security went around now snooping with their big noses and found that my father had left me a college fund. A quite generous one too. It was 50k.

My father really wanted me to become something in life since I had epilepsy. But now that they had found out about the college fund they had my family make a choice. They said, "Either you get rid of and disburse of all that money to the cent or we will take away Joseph's social security that his father left him which also included his medical insurance. This insurance coverd doctor visits, emergency visits as well as my medication.

So my family did not want to disburse the funds but had got rid of every remaining cent of the 50 thousand. They got rid of it by buying me furniture and many other things that I could live with. I was still in exile at the time and very angry and mad that the state of California would for making me do this to a person with a disability. My father just wanted me to become something in life.

During my exile, I was in and out of group homes. However, in each group home, they had one thing in common. Each one of them had a man who was a master of martial arts, and each of them taught me a different skill of martial arts.

There was this one technique called mind over matter. They all said it would help me control my seizures in a way that I never thought would be possible.

They all told me that while you're in your sleep or even if you get an ora, take the matter which is the seizure then with all the power of your mind that you could muster up, just pause for a moment. Then once the seizure tries to sneak up on you, with all the power in your mind throw the matter, the seizure, into a kind of like a fighting ring that you would see martial artists fight in or even a boxer.

After that, you picture in your mind that your mind is the strongest person in the world. It would be a very good fighter that you like in the world or anything that you could imagine that could defeat anything in the world. Once you have your figure in your mind, you crush the matter, the seizure and your seizure could go from minutes to seconds.

Your ora can be more relaxed and even at that moment though you had an ora and thought you were going to have a seizure, you just don't. So to all epileptics or to people who aren't considered epileptics but just people who have seizures, study this technique and master it.

To all parents who want their children not to have seizures by the minutes but only by the seconds, work with your children as if you were a martial arts master. I have been doing this for almost 24 years and it really works. I once noticed that love helps a lot to bring down stress and stress causes seizures. When I was loved by my girlfriend, I went five and a half months without seizures, however, once I let stress in my life from other people, I got weak. And no matter how hard I tried to take the hits or no matter how the hits came at me in life at the time, I lost that day by having a seizure.

During those five and a half months though no matter how hard the hits came at me, I was willing to take the hits and keep on going. I was not pointing at people saying he or she was stressing me out too much. Only losers do that, and I was not a loser at that time. So love your children, because if you're a person with seizures, just know all you need to survive is love. You just have to be willing to take the hits in life no matter how hard they come at you.

Some people even tried to kill me in the group homes. They tried to rape me, and they tried to even cut me by knife fighting with me, but I survived it all. They were the ones that got smashed in the walls. They were the ones that got knocked on their butts all because I knew how to fight in several ways.

After I told my family about what was happening in the group homes, they took me out immediately. Sometimes they tried to just get back at me by putting me in another one, but I still survived and showed my family who could beat who. Also I showed them who was the strongest amongst my brothers and I because they would never have survived. It was just like living in jail but with parole every now and then.

Sometime after my father's death my mother had found a man who had come to date her because he had fallen in love with her. His name was Elvis. I wasn't very thrilled at first, but we became good friends because we all had seen just how much Elvis loved our mother. Elvis did not have that great of a profession. He was a taxi driver, however, that did not matter to us only his love for our mother. Elvis had moved into our house and had become part of the family.

After my two years of exile, I finally had to go into the world on my own by living on my own because my mother had thrown me out. My first apartment was unbelievable. It was humble and livable so I tried to make a life there. In that city, I met my first love.

I found myself a roommate, but I sure found out what a roommate can do to you. One day I found my roommate in bed with her. I had beat up my friend and kicked out my girlfriend, but later on she had regretted what she had done. She had moved to live with her aunt.

Shortly after that, we had decided to get married, but it wasn't before long when that idea had gotten trashed. You see, her cousin wanted to join a Mexican gang. His initiation to become one of them was to beat me up. I was nineteen at the time and very much knowledgeable in martial arts and street fighting.

Two of the members from the Mexican gang accompanied him to see that he had done the job. I told him not to even try it, but he took a swing at me and hit me in the worst spot you could hit a person without hurting them in pure bone, my jaw. After he hit me, I turned to the others and said, "Does anyone else want to limp?" It was because I had hit her cousin and he flew six feet away with one punch.

I knew then that my first love and I could never marry. I knew because if we did, every single holiday, every future family occasion, her cousin would try to seek revenge on me for me wrecking his chance to get into Baldwin Park Northside gang.

I then went to her and her cousin's mother, and her aunt. I told them what I had done and why. I explained to her then why we could never marry. She had broken down in tears, and I told her then that I had to leave. I said, "We had to break up, and I could not come back because I was not going to take a chance on going to jail."

She begged me with tears to come back, but I had to swallow my pride, keep walking forward, and not turn around. With some help from my family, I found a place in another city in California. I lived in that city for a good number of years. There were a lot of jobs I had. I was in and out of relationships.

There were gang fights, and sometimes I had to watch my back going out the door as well as coming home. My home was an apartment somewhere on Valley Blvd.

My Friend The Bear

I WAS SEVENTEEN WHEN I SAW my first murder. My friends and I we had a friend named "The Bear". He was about nineteen years old. He was in another gang called the MOT'S. Our gang was called the Madison Oak Tree. We had a peace treaty with the MOT'S.

Then one day about a year or two later, they had a gang war with the Vuarte Rip's in 95. The Bear was just kicking back with us and we believe that they had a little peace treaty going on in another city with the Florez gang. They came out that day with about three to five members in the park right across the street where we were.

Ricardo was the leader of our gang and also my best friend. We grew up together since we were babies. He watched my back, and I watched his. Anyway, like I was saying that day, The Bear walked up not knowing that he was walking into his death. He went up to those guys and just asked them what they were doing in our city but not in any negative way.

He just asked, "What are you guys doing here in our city?" It was kind of like, what's up. Then they took out their guns that they had hidden in their jackets and shot our dear friend, "The Bear" in cold blood. They blew apart every little bit of him right in front of us and ran like cowards back to another city.

Ricardo, the leader of our gang, ordered me to stay behind because he knew my family, and he also knew that if anything would happen to me word would get around. I said I didn't care, and I wanted to go with them and avenge our dear friend. Ricardo still told me to stay behind. I would have gone if I had my own car but because these damn seizures, I will never be able to drive in my life or maybe possibly one day.

Ricardo and the rest of the gang got bats, pipes, and got all their cars, went down to a different city and avenged our dear friend. The MNG's did not know anything so we wanted to keep it that way for one reason that was because we believe there was an inside guy in the MNG's that wanted the Bear dead.

There was no other purpose for them to come out here unless someone from his own gang wanted him dead, because like I said, his until now.

Not long after when Elvis was taking me to my apartment. Once some gang members were waiting for me when I got home. I got out of Elvis's taxi and then they tried to jump me. Elvis quickly got out and had a pipe or bat, but I can't remember. That night Elvis had saved my life. I don't know if I can ever repay him for that night.

I was just going to do my best in my life and show Elvis that I can succeed in life maybe will make him happy. You see, I've noticed a kinship starting to grow between us like a father to a son. We will see. In the meantime, I'm here for him, and he's with my mother for us.

MY FRIEND'S MARRIAGE

I WAS LIVING IN A GROUP home. It was fall of 2001. I will never forget that September day. It was September 11th to be exact. I was in the kitchen when some of the group home tenants came up to me and asked me Joseph, "What's happening in the world today?" I said what do you mean? He said, "Why aren't you watching the television?"

I said to him, "Why, what happened?" He said, "You better run over here now." So I ran to the television set and there had been a terrorist attack over in New York at the twin towers. A terrorist group drove a plane right into them. So many hundreds of people, Americans, had died in an instant. And then another terrorist plane landed right into the Pentagon.

Myself being a very patriotic American, fell to my knees crying because of how many Americans had died and how many didn't have to. They called this attack "911". I then ran to the telephone dialed up my mother's home phone and told her, while I was crying, how much I loved her. I told her this because so many mothers had died and so many children were left without parents.

Myself, with my mother as my only parent, I wanted her to know how much I had felt lucky that she was still alive. I wanted to donate some blood but the Red Cross said that I was unable to because I was taking medication for my seizures. I read my bible so much that night. And ever since then, on September 11th, I play this one song by Alan Jackson called Where Were You When the World Stopped Turning on that September Day.

And that day has haunted me for quite a while because we are still at war. So many soldiers are going over there risking their lives for their country but most of them are coming home dead. It's so hard to be a patriot when you're a man with seizures. You feel helpless because there's really nothing you can do. You can't give blood to the wounded, and you can't join your fellow Americans and fight for your country.

You feel helpless and vulnerable. That's why I say that day is still haunting me and will probably haunt me the rest of my life. If you were my age or older, just like the title of that song by Alan Jackson, I would ask you where were you when the world stopped turning on that September day.

I was in my seventh year of living in another city. I went to this one Halloween dance with the Independent Living Program that I was in.

I believe around that time Brian and Manny's Mom were getting married, ironically, to a friend of mine's father. It was a friend I went to high school with. His name was Victor. He was a very easy to get along with type of guy. Victor had two little step brothers named Brian and Manny.

The Aftermath

A FTER OUR APARTMENT, I HAD moved to another. I had gotten a cozy apartment near the train tracks. I was applying for IHSS for someone to come and help clean my place up. I was also thinking at the time could there be or would there be any love in my future. And if so, how would it appear and how soon. I had many questions about my future so I went to this one fortune teller for a terra card reading.

I asked her about my future love, money and life. She told me about my future and my loves. They will have both my mother and dads spirits in them. My finance future will be big, and I will be very wealthy, rich, and also famous. My life will be very long, and I will live to my 90's or to my 100's.

I asked her, "When will my next girlfriend be around?" She said, "You will hear three knocks on your door tomorrow, and this woman will lead you to your next girlfriend."

I thought right, whatever you say but then a scary thing happened the next day. I woke up to three knocks on my apartment door, and there was no more no less than three knocks. A lady was at the door. She was my IHSS worker named Anna. I was very depressed that day so I just kept staring at the wall from my couch.

She asked me, "What was wrong?" I said, "See that spot on the wall. That is my girlfriend." And then Anna said, "That's horrible, Joseph. I think I can help." She said, "She had a God daughter which was her niece, Anna. She was named after me and that she was single too. I'm going to hook both of you up."

I could not believe what I heard at the time because of what the psychic lady had said with the terra cards. It's the one thing she had predicted to the letter. The psychic lady said, "That this woman would have the characteristics of both my mother and my father because she saw the stubbornness of a woman in my family." Now that would be my mother.

And then she said, "That this woman had the birth sign of July which my father was born in. I met her that very evening. She was simple, but I only tried to tell her at the time that I heard that being overweight can cause heart attacks. I was not trying to judge her at all or even make fun of her.

But she, with her stubbornness, thought that I was making fun of her. It wasn't long before we kept walking back and forth from my apartment to her mother's apartment. One evening she had a heart attack, and she fell into my arms. Luckily at the time, I was a security officer and had taken CPR and first aid.

I had saved her life using CPR until the paramedics showed up. They checked out her heart to see how fast her heart was racing. And then they said, "If I had not performed CPR, she would have been dead because her heart almost stopped." Her mother and family had thanked me for saving her daughter's life, and her sister's life, and so on and so forth.

Her mother then said to her and her sister, who was a little heavy, "You better get both your buts over to the gym and start trimming down." I said to her mother and my girlfriend, "See I told you I was not trying to make fun of you. I was just telling you what I heard."

Her mother thanked me by having me move in with them. So I was staying with my girlfriend in her room and coincidently, her mother and I share the same birthday, March 19th. My girlfriend was a very stubborn girl though. If I even tried to go and get the mail, she would hang onto my leg like a led weight. Then she would say, "You're going to go to the bar and try to find another woman, another bitch, aren't you; even though I never cheated on her or looked at any other woman.

I found out from her mother that she had anger management classes she went to. And coincidently, she was bipolar like my ex-wife. I tried to have a family with my girlfriend, but then her mother told me another secret. She said, "She had her tubes tied and was unable to have children." I said and asked, "How can she have periods if she has her tubes tied?" It seems as though after her mother found out that I was her first, they went to the hospital and then got her tubes tied without even my consent.

It wasn't that we were married at the time, but it's just that I wanted to have children with her daughter, but her mother would not allow it because of having hereditary family problems. I was with my girlfriend for three years, and I decided to leave because these problems started getting really heavy on me.

She would do crazy things, and a couple times, she even hit me. One time I had to restrain her up against the wall to try and calm her down. She tried to break through, and I had to restrain her again before she did something out of control to me. When her mother found out, she took this one picture of me that was hanging in my girlfriend's room. This one picture that my sister had made very large.

It was a picture that I had taken at a modeling studio when my father was still alive sometime when I was about fourteen, sometime before he died. Her mother busted it in half and threw it in the garbage. I could not believe what her mother had done even after I had told her mother what her daughter was doing and that I had no choice but to defend myself and hit her.

So that's why I had decided to leave because no one in that house was sane. My girlfriend begged me and begged me to forgive her and stay, but I told my girlfriend I had given you three years of forgiveness and yet you still did the same thing. It's not because you are trying to change but because you can't change.

So I left her, and I did not turn my back to even look at her. I moved to my mother's then and lived with my mother temporarily. Things weren't working out between my mother and I so then my younger brother found me a place by looking at some ads in the Penny Saver.

It seems there was an apartment that was just for my budget over in Riverside. I was again with the regional center only it was the Inland Regional Center which is an independent living program.

It was sometime around Christmas of that year 2003 that I had spoken to my only living grandparent my mama's father. He had been very ill for quite sometime. When I got onto that phone, tears were falling like rain from my face, and my polish was pouring out of my mouth as if I was fluent already in it.

I remember the first words that came out of my mouth. In polish, I had asked him, "Is this my grandfather?" I know I should have asked him, is this my grandfather? But for someone who had never spoken to a grandparent ever in his life, I was a little nervous. If this makes any sense. And then he responded back in Polish to me saying, "Yes, this is your grandfather."

And then my grandfather asked me, "Is this my little Joseph? The one that has to suffer so much from seizures?" I replied in Polish, "Yes my grandfather." My sister and my mother started crying because they knew this was a heart-touching moment between both my grandfather and myself.

There were other questions asked and also responded to in the conversation. After I had my chance to speak with my grandfather and said our I love you's, I made one promise just before the phone went to my mother. The promise was to remember this forever, and he asked me to make something out of myself and become something more than my brothers so that I would be able to show my brothers that I'm not just someone with seizures.

You see, I had told him that my brothers sometimes pick on me about having to take care of me. They would have to try and help me, I told him. So he said, "Promise me you'll make something of yourself." I really didn't understand why except that it was because he loved me so much.

Two years later I understood. It was that he was saying his goodbyes because he had died. He died at 93. He lived a very good long life and what I'm doing now is writing this book and going to go to college to become a doctor of geology. I'm not going to do it for myself but for my grandfather.

Two years later after his death, my aunt came from Poland and made a shocking visit at our doorstep. I did not know at first who this lady was, but she knew me when she cried out my name, Joseph. And she said my cousin, Joshzek, or translated in English, Andrew. She had spoken in

Polish after I had questioned, yes, I am your aunt, Wicia translated to Vicky or Victoria.

I quickly shouted, Mama! Mama! I ran outside and gave my aunt, who came all the way from Poland to America, a hug and a kiss because I only knew my aunt Wicia from the telephone. I had also only knew some of my cousins from talking to them on the telephone. So when I was outside and she said in Polish, "This is my son, Joshzek." She translated to Andrew.

I grabbed him and gave him a bear hug because I had never seen him before in my life either. When I hugged both of them, all I said at the same time was, "My God," in Polish. And then I told them in Polish, "I've been praying for this day." My mother did not know why I was shouting for her. I suppose she thought I just wanted her to help me with something else or to bother her with something.

Because when she was coming down the hall, she was yelling, "What the hell do you want from me?" My mother then turned so red and embarrassed because I said in Polish to my mother, "I don't want you. Your sister wants you." She responded, and shouted in Polish, "Oh my God, Wicia."! And then I said to her in Polish, "What were you saying to me? What were you saying to me with my hand over my ear?"

She told me in Polish to be quiet and those two sisters started screaming and crying and hugging and kissing. It was a heart-felt moment. We went to the beach all day and took pictures. I bought a music box that played the tune, Can't help falling in love by Elvis Presley. I wound up the music box and let the tune play. Then I sang to my aunt the song.

There were some happy tears over the song I sang to her. This is something Joshzek/Josh would probably never do for his mama. I believe he was very jealous. I gave the music box to her and told her to keep it.

I believe my cousin expected more than a music box from his cousins because our father, when he was alive, would send apple boxes filled with gifts from America to Poland. So to my cousin, it was like that's it, a music box? No money? No gifts? I believe he was quite disappointed, but I can't say that for sure.

I will never forget that day when we took them to the airport, LAX, to catch their flight. It was so hard to say goodbye without crying. I know that there's hardly a time wh en a man cries. But after seeing somebody you never knew before, like my grandfather, just talking to him over the phone, it's hard not to. Tears were falling out like rain again.

While we were hugging, kissing, and saying goodbye, I just wanted to I wanted to grab both of them and say you're not going anywhere. It felt for me like either you stay here or I'm going with you. It was the same for my mother. I wished at that moment that I could have pulled out of pocket a million dollars and just forget my life over here.

And then take my mother and I along with them just like that. I was very upset that we were still a pour and struggling family. That's why after they left I made a solemn vow that no matter what woman came into my life; no matter how hard life will hit me that I will make something of myself. I will be rich so that if we were ever stuck in this sort of situation again, I could take the money of my pocket and just leave.

It's been eight years since that moment. I'm going to college and my major is geology. It's a rough ride right now because the financial aid is only covering my classes. I have to cover my books, and my job as a bartender is not going well right now. The company that gives me the leads isn't working out because not many people are looking for a bartender in my area.

Also when they do want a bartender in my area, I give them negotiable quotes and the people that need a bartender don't get back to me. And if they do get back to me, the answer is never mind or job is taken. There is always a negative response. I find it very weird and stressful because here I am a bartender, and I'm giving them a negotiable quote such as what would you like to pay me or we could work out a negotiable price, but I don't here back from them.

Other bartenders for the same company give one quote and one quote only and seem to get hired. But with me, I'm always willing to negotiate and hear what people can afford. They always seem to take other bartenders. I'm considered a silver star bartender but still trying to get hired.

I should be charging a lot more and not being negotiable but have a set wage. And yet I still try to negotiate for people. So far it's been a long road of hope, but I keep myself very optimistic. I also am saving every single cent that I can. Hopefully this book can make some dreams come true. This book is only the beginning. There are many more books to come.

I had never spoken of this until now because I was to keep it a secret until my mother's death, but she's dying and is very ill. How can I keep it a secret anymore. it's out and for everyone to know that I was the only one amongst my brothers to have spoken to him before he died.

The Gold Diggers

A FTER MY AUNT LEFT, I had moved out, but I did not like living alone. I also was single at the time so I got on a dating site for a while." In the long run, I met a woman named Mary. We were chatting for about six months to about a year. Mary was a teacher or so she said. Mary and I did online dating and that's how we got to know each other. She spoke to me about an ex-boyfriend psycho stalking her. So since I always had an open heart and was very brave, the bravest one amongst all my brothers and in my family, I said, "Come and live with me if you want to, and I'll protect you.

So Mary moved in. I said though one condition, "This is a 50/50 relationship. If you live here, you pay half the rent and half the utilities. She said, "don't worry I'll get a job as soon as I get there." She would quit her job as a teacher that she already had and moved in. I took her word for it.

The first month I had her looking for work but nothing. Second month comes around and nothing. Six months came by and still no job yet. I finally found myself forced to find a job for her because the Inland Regional Center and my Independent Living Program counselor said that they would inform the authorities if she didn't get work.

I found out earlier in my life when I had first moved out over into West Covina, a friend of mine had a girl living with him and he was receiving social security. They told him that if someone moves in with you they are to be working and help with the bills.

Once the federal government found out that she wasn't working, he was told she could be put in prison. He didn't want this to happen, but they put her in a federal prison because by law, if you live with someone who receives social security they must be working to help with bills. You cannot just expect your boyfriend or girlfriend who is receiving any kind of state income to pay for everything.

I tried explaining this to Mary for six months, and she thought that I was just kidding around. All she was doing those six months was just living off of me and my love. So I mentioned the situation to Mary that the Inland Regional Center and my independent living program were going to inform the federal government and she was going to be arrested unless she got a job.

So I helped get her a job fast working for the IHSS which is called the In Home Supported Services Program. After she got the job, she refused to pay half the rent where we lived. She only paid the bills and not the rent. I told her every month what the consequences would be even if she had a job. All she said was, "I'm paying the bills and I'm buying the groceries."

I said, "It's your job to pay the groceries. Now as far as paying for them, I'm giving you the $60.00. You're not paying all the bills. I'm paying the full rent, the electric bill, and all you're paying is the gas and your stupid phone bill." She said, "Well I need that phone." I said, "You make $500.00 every two weeks.

I'm the one that got you this job, and I got it for you so you could stay out of a federal prison."

I said, "What the hell do you do with the rest of the money?" Mary said, "I'm buying nice clothes to look sexy for you, and I buy you nice things." I said, "Well I don't want no more nice things. I want half the rent, and since I take care of the groceries, I need you to start paying for the electric bill too."

She said, "But the electric bill is in your name." I said, "It don't matter because you could give me the cash to the hand, and I'll take care of that bill." Mary then said to me, "No, you're going to spend it." I said to Mary, "Do you think I actually want my credit ruined or do you want the lights cut off along with any power that they will cut off." She said, "Put the electric bill in my name, and I'll take care of it."

I then told Mary, "That can't happen because the gas bill has come already two or three times with late payments, and they cut off our gas. Also I needed to go with my independent living counselor and take care of it. I told her you are not responsible enough to have any of these accounts in your name." Mary said, "No, you just want my money to go and spend on foolish things.

I said to Mary, "Foolish things? Who's the one buying these sexy lingeries and these dresses, and who's the one going and buying makeup and jewelry. I told her then I guess I will have to call the federal government, and you'll have to go to jail. It's a federal prison for women." Then Mary said, "Okay, I'll start taking care of things." My family, the Inland Regional Center, and my independent living counselor said, "You are going to regret trusting her."

And I did regret trusting her because she did not pay the other half of the rent in the upcoming month. She did not pay the other bills that she was supposed to pay either, and the electric and gas bill I put in her name just like she had requested. Everything she had promised got us removed from that apartment.

So we then had to rent a room in a house in the same city, the landlord got very angry but not with me. He hollered at Mary. And Mary said, "Joseph the landlord hollered at me." I said, can you blame him? I told you you're not responsible and you don't pay the bills. You're going to have bill collectors yelling at you, and you're going to have landlords evict you. I told her he's not angry with me because I've tried to pay all the rent, and he's knows that you have a job."

He offered me to be able to stay here alone. I said, "She is my girlfriend." He said, "To dump you and to get a new girlfriend, a better one, and a more responsible one.", So we tried a third time, and this time, we were renting a room in Parris CA. I believe that's in San Bernardino County too

Now this landlord was really crazy, and he was eastern Indian, I believe. He had a very beautiful wife. There was only one thing that went wrong in that house. That was the fact that they had a gay guy renting who was making friends with my girlfriend, Mary. He was having her paint his toenails and giving him hugs and kisses on the cheek.

Mary told me this and I got very angry because it seemed as though he was hitting on my girlfriend because he was giving her kisses on the cheek, and hugs. He was also asking her to paint his toenails and that sounded really crazy to me. So I went next door to him and I said, "Stay away from my girlfriend. I know that you're gay but that does not mean that you could take advantage of my girlfriend and monopolize her time when she could be spending it with me."

This guy said to me, "Mary can hug and kiss whoever she wants." So that was it for me. Mary never really had seen me jealous until the next day when I waited until he got out of the shower. Then in front of Mary I said to the guy, "Hey!" Then I socked him as hard as I could. He then ran into his room saying that's it, Mary. Your boyfriend's dead.

He came out to fight me, but I took a punch then took him head first down the stairs. So every step down his head would hit hard, and he got it good.

The landlord's wife saw me to be very handsome and more handsome than her own husband. She was speaking with Mary and asked how the sex was. Mary told her everything, and the landlord's wife said to Mary, "If she could have a taste of me?" You know we could, get a threesome going, but I never agreed. However, her husband heard about how much his wife liked me. So he got real angry with me because he thought that I was flirting with his wife when it was the other way around so he asked us to get our stuff and get the hell out. We got our things together in less than a month and moved back to Riverside.

Once we got another apartment, I was not going to take Mary's tricky crap anymore so this time I got back at her. After the first month I got ahold of my brother, Greg and told him I was putting everything in her name. I also let him know that I needed help moving back to our moms place. I packed fast, but most of my stuff was still in boxes.

Greg came, and we left quickly so she would need to pay everything or be evicted this upcoming month. I told management I was moving because she was having somebody else move in this upcoming month and that we were breaking up. It left her with all the responsibility and me free and clear.

I had gotten back at that back stabbing witch. During our relationship, she cheated on me with that so-called stalking ex-boyfriend that tried to kill me with his white Camaro.

Now I was back with my mother, Elvis, and my brother Greg. Elvis did not like Mary anyways. He was right that she was no good and to watch out.

THE WOMAN WHO I NEVER KNEW

Could Touch My Heart

JADE

I MET MY FRIEND RICARDO AGAIN. He had two girls in his life. His friend named Sandra had a friend nine years older than me named, Jade. Ricardo described Jade all wrong. He described Jade like a rich princess with a beautiful heart.

Now looks can be deceiving at first, but I still arrived with a dozen red roses. She had brown hair and very beautiful. She was an older woman. I then whispered in Ricardo's ear. You did not describe her to me like this. I brought her a dozen red roses. We all went out on our first date after Jade had changed.

Now on our second date, some things went wrong. I had wanted to break it off with Jade before things had gotten too deep, but we made up that night. We started out just dating, but dating a lot. Then we jumped into moving into an apartment together. Our first apartment was in Tulsa.

In that apartment we found our true love for each other. Things went great, and we were finally on our own. Jade gave me five and a half months of love and without seizures. I almost was able to drive, but she gave me a gift instead. Jade showed me that my theory was true that my seizures are only stress related. Also with true love and medication, my seizures can be controlled.

The day I had the seizure that stopped what could have been six months in a row. It is what was needed in order to get to drive, but I went only five and a half months. Jade and I had an argument the night before. I went for a walk with her to Mc Donald's and back the next day. On the way back home, I fell into the street with a seizure. The first attack during the day in a long time, but nevertheless, it was a seizure and stress related.

We still loved each other. They say sometimes bad things happen, but you can still get hurt or just fake it. You should swallow your pride because love is worth it and that's forever.

I'm not saying Jade and I did not have our share of arguments. Heck, we sometimes broke up in that place, but got back together four times in that Tulsa apartment. But one thing that drove us out, actually two things, the landlord and the constant fighting of the neighbors. So we gave our 30 day notice and then moved to a place which we now regret.

Once we moved there, the landlord and landlady were both renting out to crazy people. We both could not believe it. Not only were the renters crazy, but the landlords themselves were also crazy.

There was one guy who hit on my lady, Jade. I almost decked the guy because of what Jade had told me. He told Jade that he wanted to know if she would get it on with him in his room. She got so angry with Sam that she told him that she would not do that with him. He actually had the audacity to ask her why not. She told him that she was with Joseph. He still kept saying come on and let's do it anyways and then Sam started yelling at Jade.

My lady, Jade, got up and went into my room to talk to me and let me know what was said. I became furious and called the landlady and landlord. I suggested to Jade that she call her brothers and let them know what had happened because she was so furious. They were very angry at that psycho, Sam.

Jade's brothers' came out to talk to Sam, and Sam became very irate with Jade's brothers and very intimidated. He mouthed off at her brothers and pretended to try and hit them both. Both her brothers talked him down and told him to leave her alone and also not to ask their sister to buy beer for him. It was not her responsibility to buy his beer.

Later, the landlady and landlord came to talk with Sam about the situation, and he lied to them and said, "Jade took me seriously about what was said." Sam said he was not serious about anything he said to Jade, and that just wasn't true. He tried to make Jade look bad by saying that none of it was true.

However, I overheard every rotten thing Sam was saying to the landlords about my lady and her brothers. I spoke to the landlords later on and mentioned every single thing that I heard tearing Jade apart. I said, "Why do you think Jade would actually be crying and then come to me? On top of that, why do you think we would actually call her brothers to speak with him if everything were not true?

I said to them, "He smokes pot in the house, he drinks beer, and he's nothing but a liar." The next day we had to call the landlords again because this time Sam was out to get all of us. I said to them, "I overheard Sam talking to someone over the phone and in great detail about getting rid of us. He also had said in great detail that there was a guy with his girlfriend that got him in trouble with her brothers and the landlords. He also said he would pay to take them all out and get rid of them, whatever had to be done just do it.

The boyfriend, the girlfriend, and the landlords said, "Screw them all, they're done. I want them all gone." A couple times after that we saw a car going up and down the street looking at our particular house. And when we went out, we would see the same car following us. We weren't sure if it was Sam following us or a friend of his.

We were all terrified after hearing this phone conversation so I called the police to check out the situation. The police came and knocked on Sam's bedroom door during the middle of the night, and Sam did not want to come out and talk to the police. They kept pounding and pounding on Sam's door and finally he came out.

Sam just complained of Jade and I being together, and he was not happy about the living arrangements regarding us. He told them that we stole stuff from his room which was not true because his room was always locked. We don't do that anyways. We couldn't even do that if we wanted to because we don't know how to pick a lock. The police said to Sam, "If you don't like the living arrangement, why don't you stop complaining and just move." Sam had plenty of money to move but he said, "Why don't they move."

They said, "Probably because they can't afford it since the boyfriend is on Social Security, and she is low income. So the next day came, and we told the landlords about the police, and about the car following us, and the continuous marijuana smoking inside the house. So they gave Sam a two week notice and kicked him out of the house.

After Sam was gone, his room became mine and another tenant moved into my old room. This was a crazy old lady named Moria. We couldn't really get along with Moria either because she was crazy too. Basically, it was a crazy house so we looked around for a new apartment because Jade talked me into it since she couldn't take the madness anymore.

We gave our landlords a thirty day notice even before we found a place because we were that determined to get out of there. We had many break ups between Jade and I because of everything that had happened, but we got back together.

After the thirty days, we had moved to a nice apartment complex in Upland, Ca. Once we moved into Upland, Ca, our lives were going to change like never before, and we didn't even know it. In the summer time, I saw how great Jade was in her bathing suit since we had a swimming pool and a Jacuzzi. We went swimming a lot and also went into the Jacuzzi. That year after we had moved something terrible happened.

Even though things started to look great for us, and I was showing my true feelings for Jade, there was something on Jade's chest growing. And actually, a couple of marks that looked like chicken pox that started to come onto Jade's body. They first appeared like pimples but then when they got a little bit bigger, Jade took herself to see this one Mexican doctor who really didn't know a thing about the practice of medicine. He was horrible.

Even though it looked like chicken pox that guy told my lady, Jade that it was some sort of a fungus. Jade explained to the doctor that it started out the size of a pimple on her chest and then her face. He told Jade that nothing had to be done about it. Jade's Aunt Rachel asked if there was any kind of a cream or antibiotic she could take, and he said, "No." It was just like saying take two of these and call me in the morning. That's the kind of doctor he was.

My Knowledge Of Seizures

I KNOW A LOT ABOUT doctors because I grew up with seizures as I said before. And now I'm thirty eight years old, and I have so much knowledge about epilepsy, seizures, doctors, and medications that I would like to share with the world. Since I know I'm there are parents out there who are just starting out with a child, whether it be a baby or their kid going to grade school, that are starting to have seizures and they don't know what to do.

I'm not saying I'm a doctor, but I can give you some advice from what I have studied on computers and books. I can give you my philosophies and my knowledge. One, if you have a baby that is about six months old that is just starting out with seizures, you would definitely need to check the family background. The same goes for a child to about six years old because seizures are something that can be like any other illness such as cancer, diabetes etc.

These illnesses can skip a generation. Your grandparents could have had it and then maybe your father, mother, aunts and uncles. They might not have had any signs or even any illnesses. However, just by chance, without you knowing that any of your grandparents had this, all the sudden your child just develops it. Always make sure that before you have a child, you check and ask your parents or grandparents if there's any illnesses in your family's background.

Two, if your child is anywhere from six months two years old, definitely check what blood type he or she has. Your blood type can determine just how much and what kind of medication your child can take if they want to put your child on medication. se I had a very low blood type and these idiot doctors gave me a very strong medication called Depakote when I was about a year or two old.

I almost died because the medication stopped my breathing. It was a very strong drug for a child my age. That kind of drug would be for a child maybe four to six years or older. It can help but not for a baby. There are many kinds of seizures out there. A baby would most likely have petite mall seizures which would be a very low kind of seizure and common kind for a baby.

Other seizures are called febrile seizures which would be a seizure with a fever. Usually they come with high fever and sometimes the fever can be so monstrous that you would have to take your child and put him or her into ice water. I know this from experience, and I would scream and cry while my siblings and my mother would be carrying me kicking and screaming to the bathtub filled with ice water.

After febrile seizures, I developed the worse kind of seizure that a person could have which is grand mall. After my father died, I was kicked out of my home and left on my own. I studied and studied and studied because I knew there had to be some way to control them. I believe I said earlier in my book that I learned this method called mind over matter. It's where you take the matter which would be the seizure in your mind and you use your mind to overcome it. Your mind just says that you are in control.

Even though I had the worst kind of seizure, using this method I was able to cut down my seizures from minutes to just seconds. They never came back by using this method during the day. I have now what they would call nocturnal seizures. That means they only occur in my sleep. I impressed eleven of the best neurologists in the state of California at the UCLA Medical Center because they did not believe me.

So if you have a child, try to give him or her all the love you can that's what I learned. If you want to fight with your child or have some sort of argument, try and have one of you just walk it off. Just think to yourself is your argument more important than your child having a seizure or would you want your child to have seizures for the rest of his or her life. I found out that seizures can be psychosematic which means the seizures can be brought on psychologically due to any arguments in the household or even on the playground or in any stressful situation.

So try and love your child and each other. Live a stress free life because I am living a stress free life right now. I have love from my girlfriend. And even though I may have negativity from my family saying that I may never have a great career, I blow it over my shoulder. Also even though I may have a lot of homework to become who I want to be in life, I don't let it get to me. I say to myself that I will do it and become who I want to be in life and that all I need is love and affection.

Then I remember a phrase that my father taught me. He taught me that if anyone including my family or anyone that would put me down, just say to yourself that all you need is me, myself, and I. These are the words of wisdom for almost thirty nine years of having seizures.

So if a doctor tells you that your son or daughter has epilepsy, do not believe it at first. Epilepsy is more like an illness in the brain and seizures are just from time to time. Sometimes though, doctors they try and convince parents that their child has epilepsy and the only sure fire cure is operation or this one thing called a vagal nerve stimulator.

I tried the vagal nerve stimulator and they said it was the latest in technology but all it caused me was minor heart attacks. The operation they have you should never take it because they will say that they can take the seizures away or the epilepsy. However, all you'll get is very negative side effects.

One, you could possibly come out there with no seizures, but you will have loss of hair for the rest of your life on one half of your head. And if it does grow in, it will grow in and it won't grow the same. Second, you could come out with mental retardation for the rest of your life or you could even die on e table. That's why you should never accept the operation.

JADE'S DIFFICULTIES

THIS DOCTOR FOR MY GIRLFRIEND said, "He was going to have a biopsy done on the lumps in her neck because she had developed some lumps there." There were two that felt just like bee bees lodged in her neck and a couple of other lumps that were near them. There was also one that was about the size of a golf ball growing on her collar bone, and she was running fevers every single day. They were getting worse by the minute. It was very heartbreaking for me to watch her go through this. I couldn't take it anymore.

She developed something on her upper chest and on the left side of the face. There were many on the face and she felt like giving up because she didn't want people to see her this way. Especially me, the love of her life. She wanted to stay home and hide away from people and even me. She didn't feel like she was beautiful to me anymore even though I would always tell her she was, and oh God, to me she would always be.

Taking care of Jade was very challenging and very difficult. I almost found myself lost and could have gone into another exile because I didn't know how to handle this even though I loved her. But rather than going into exile again, I read books and poems to take my mind off of what Jade was going through. Jade had many tears over this. I tried very hard to console her and many 911 trips to the hospital.

MY INTERPRETATION OF CHI AND BRUCE LEE'S POEM

That Helped Me From Exile

ONE OF THE POEMS THAT I had read to keep myself from going into exile was written by Bruce Lee. It was about what Kung Fu went through in his mind. And if I share it with you, you can see how it helped me from going into exile. It kept me very calm and not stressed out. It reads Kung Fu is more than a system of fighting. It's a system of thought. You must out think your opponent in whatever form he takes because some of them will be more than just men.

We all have inner demons to fight. We call these demons fear and hatred and anger. For example, if you don't conquer them, you will have a life of a hundred years is a tragedy. If you do, a life of

A single day can be a triumph. That was one of the books that I read and studied. The Book of CHI is another one that I really got into, mastered and studied.

The Book of CHI teaches us to free yourself to make light your burden. The past makes us who we are. Don't make it your burden. Lower your burden and run towards a new life. This is the Book of CHI Life, Energy. Not a manual of martial arts. When you are confused, it can bring you peace. One, gather energy together, but don't use force. Force will not break it. The Book of CHI is so refined that it teaches us to avoid killing the enemy but make best use of every opportunity.

Two, you break it without force. You use the power of air and water. No fancy tricks or the flow will cease. The air current should match the universe. No desire, no lust, no immovable roots. No stirring of dust. There is only the way of nature. This is called TAI CHI. Three, keep yourself the center of gravity and utilize the attackers force. A spinning ball repels other objects. It touches, yet itself stands steady and firm.

Even in movement, there is always stillness. No matter how hard I push the ball, the water springs it back. So the stronger you are, the stronger your opponent. Because I can't even defeat the still water. Four, so what is natural is everything in nature. Taoism teaches us to avoid disaster and to to not resist. Taoism also teaches us to help other people. You should know the importance of doing nothing.

If you have a heart, how can you do nothing? A true Taoist gives up his own life in order to avoid the deaths of more innocents. You must be prepared to die. Because if so, it's fate. If you can't stand firm, how can you attack? Use the attackers force to strike. My hands do not have strength and power. My heart embraces peace and calm. Resigning myself to avoid adversity. Seeing richness out of the void.

Violence be turned to peace. There are always guiding fates. Dynamic or still, divided or multiply. Follow fate to go in and out of the mortal world. Merciless is mercy. Follow your heart and not be aggressive for merciless is mercy. Everything has a life including the plants. We mustn't damage the life of another just for our own gain. This is too selfish.

Every blow of the Shaolin fist must be forceful. Each move is a surprise to the enemy. It must be swift as the wind. These are the basics of the Shaolin fist. You must be steadfast in every situation. To achieve the highest level, your body must be as hard as steel. Strike first to prevent attack. Maintain a steady stance. Buddhist Palm The key is in how you breathe.

This is how I survived the stress of Jade's beginning of the doctors and their horrible and continuous disregard of her real situation which I will be explaining. She went to a different doctor after that and he said, "He was going to put in a referral for a surgeon to have the thing on her chest looked at." They submitted the paperwork and it got denied a few days later.

THE CANCER NEWS

S HE CALLED THE INSURANCE TO find out why it got denied and they said it was because the doctor did not give any notes regarding the problem and they also put wrong information on the referral regarding Jade. Jade called to find out if they can resubmit the paperwork on a rush basis and they were going to work on it but suggested that she go to the hospital to see if they can do anything.

Jade's aunt Rachel took her to the hospital and the doctor there told Jade that her insurance would not do anything about the thing growing on her chest because it's cosmetic. Jade was in tears once again because no one would help her and it kept getting bigger.

I called the doctor's office to put some fear in them because I saw my lady going through hell. I saw my lady waking up every single morning next to me with bloody sheets from what was growing on her chest and face. And then I find out that they said at the hospital, "They could do nothing for her when they handle people every day for everything and anything."

So I finally had threated them that I would get the best attorney I could find and sue them with a wrongful mal-practicing lawsuit if they did not start treating my lady. The same day we got a call from the doctor saying my lady got the authorization to go and see a surgeon, Dr. Mullen.

I called Dr. Mullen because my lady, Jade, told me how much pain she was in and that the thing on her chest and face was growing every twenty four hours. I spoke to Dr. Mullen and told him the situation. The doctor said, "To get her to the hospital immediately." So I called her aunt Rachel and told her that the doctor said to bring her in stat.

Her aunt Rachel did not wait no twenty four hours. She took her niece right away and under doctor's orders, she got admitted to the hospital. And thanks to my help and pursuance from learning this from both my father and mother, she had the biopsy the next evening. So I had done the impossible. Unfortunately, the news came two weeks later about the results from the biopsy that my love had cancer and stage 4.

The oncologist came to see my lady and said, "She had to start chemo right away and it would be for three days in a row. She would have to take four different kinds of chemo the first day and then one chemo the second and third day. They gave her medicine before the treatment to ease the suffering of chemo.

After the chemo treatment she had to stay a little longer at the hospital due to her white cell counts and platelets going too low. Once she got released from the hospital, she went to stay at her mom's house instead of living with her aunt. And me, I moved in with my mom while she was going through this. She needed as much help as possible from her mother and a little space from me.

Though I loved her dearly, we saw each other whenever we could. But during those treatments, I had to let her rest.

My Father's Life Lessons

I T WAS THE FALL SEMESTER of 2014. I had started late registration but just in time to get one class. It was Counseling 156. Counseling 156 was just the class I needed to start my life over again. Its focus and main objective in the class was to direct me for the classes that I needed to take for my major. My major was geology.

I was doing this, not just for myself, but for a promise that I made about 24 years ago to my father before he died. My father wanted me to be somebody in life, and he taught me many life's lessons. Growing up I learned a lot of old sayings from my father. Like I said earlier, "I was not one to listen."

I went out a lot and got into trouble. I was a free spirit. But when I came home, my father always had sayings for me. He even had sayings for me before I went out. The same thing went to Greg, Victoria and Henry too. Our father did this all so that we could grow up very wise and know the meanings of the sayings later on in life.

Also by the time that we knew the meanings to the sayings, we could pass the sayings onto our children and it would go on in the circle of life. It would go on from father to son, and father to daughter but sometimes it may have to go from uncle to nephew or grandfather to grandson. That way it could fall back into the circle of life.

Some fathers would not teach their sons or would not have the time to. So in order to prevent a crack in the chain, it would have to be taught by the male members of the family. Some Calkowskis' would have told the female Calkowskis', such as my aunts because they did not really know the sayings so basically the men in my family were the wisest.

Not to say that the females did not get a talking to, but they just did not know them all. For instance, my father would say when I wanted to go out instead of staying home and doing some chores, "You'll get what you deserve." And just like my father said, "If I went out or anyone of us went out without our father's consent, wouldn't you know it, something bad would happen to us."

Then when any of us came home our father would say, "See you got what you deserved." Another saying that my father had was the famous "I told you so." Another saying was not to ask stupid questions because my father always said, "You ask a silly question, you'll always get a silly answer." This one saying used to make me angry at first because I was only a little kid. But it cheered me up too.

He would use it even when I was a toddler when I was crying in his arms. So sometimes he would cry with me, and say, "Don't cry, Joseph. Things always look better on the other side." So then I would laugh and just look at my father and learn and heed those words. Don't look a gift horse in the mouth was another one of my father's sayings.

There's a meaning behind this saying that I found out from my father. It's to never expect a poor person or a working family member to give you or get you anything you may want for your birthday or Christmas. There were many other sayings that he said such as, "If I thought I could do something in an easy way instead of a hard way, my father would always say, show me I'm from Missouri.'

This was his way of teaching all of us even our mother that life will always be hard and that there's no easy way out. Also what you start you have to finish was another famous saying of his. And to make sure in life that if we started a job, school, or any kind of an important task, it would show us never to give up.

I guess that's why everything worked out so well between Elvis and my mother. It's also why I want to show Elvis just what I can do as much as my mother. Because I want Elvis to be just as proud of me as my family. Because to me Elvis is not just a friend anymore, but family.

Also I want to show Elvis that I can do things because I believe he loves me just as much as my mother dose. Because he sure has shown how proud he can be towards me and so I shall always cherish that.

And in December of 2012, we had an addition to our family. You see that year our older brother Henry had gotten married and in December came another little Calkowski, Augustin is his name coincidently. He was born on the 21st just like his father's birthdate in August. Also coincidently, they named him Augustin as almost the spelling of the month August?

Augustin is now almost three, but this past December we were shocked to hear that Helena, that's Henrys wife's name, is having another little Calkowski in August of this year 2015. It was a surprise.

Finally, he also said, "The way you make your bed is the way you're going to sleep in it." Behind this saying, I learned that if you try to do things in life and you mess up then it's going to be your responsibility to fix the situation. You can't point to anyone else and say that, "He or she needs to do it. That it's you and yourself alone."

All these life lessons that my father taught me I will never forget. That's why I'm continuing to go to college. I'm thirty eight and I'm going to be thirty nine in March, and I will not finish until I am a geologist to make my father proud. And to show everyone in my family that say I will not finish that I am going to do anything and everything to finish what I started.

My father gave me three aspects of his life to make me the student I am today which were hardworking, rules, and my environment. One rule I've learned through my father is to take on the A college writing café for success in my classes. Another rule I remember is, that if we weren't working hard, our father would have us watch the fruit tree workers work like slaves and go through blood, sweat, and tears. I didn't enjoy this, but my father wanted to teach us a lesson.

In order to show us a hardworking life, my father would give us chores to do to earn money. My father would have my brothers and I work by pulling weeds, cutting grass with a push mower, cutting hedges with hand hedge cutters and cutting palm trees with hand saws. It was hard work, but we had to do this to earn money.

The environment our father raised us in was hard because he wanted to show us a hardworking life. The environment was not a business community yet so the work was limited to two jobs only which was door-to-door sales, and working in the fruit fields. Sometimes we would not even get an allowance, but if we showed that we worked hard, then he gave us the money. I remember if we asked our father for an allowance he would say, "I allow you to sleep here, and I allow you to eat here." He was a very strict father but very loving. I am who I am today because of my father.

They say the past can haunt you or make the best of you. They also say the past makes you who you are. And as Malcolm X once said, "The mind is a terrible thing to waste." I've been reading upon Malcolm X's life and what he did to make him who he was. Because just like me, he was a man that came from the streets. He did not know how to write or read at first. But yet, he had a mentor, Mohammed.

And once, Malcolm X spent some time in prison. He was doing everything he could to make himself a very knowledgeable man by reading dictionaries from the very beginning to the very end. He also practiced his writing skills so that he could actually write a letter to Mohammed. I envy that kind of spirit in a man. I just wish a lot of our younger generation today that think they cannot write or read would follow in Malcolm X's footsteps and philosophy – a mind is a terrible thing to waste.

And just like Malcolm X had a solemn goal to be able to communicate with his mentor, Mohammed I now have a solemn goal. Because eight years ago when my Aunt Vica and cousin were leaving I said to them, "I would do whatever it takes "WHATEVER" to be able to bring myself, my mother, and my family out there to see them.

I then thought of everything I could possibly do in life and everything I felt I was good at. I then said to myself I need to go back to school. I tried in 2009 but then I never finished. I tried to work harder but the economy kept getting worse. It started to lay me off or should I say hire me and then lay me off again. I felt like I was getting nowhere.

For eight years, I've been trying to get somewhere in life, but like my father always used to say, "You're getting nowhere fast." I finally knew what I had to do. I had to go back to school.

So I started college in the fall of 2014. My class was called Counseling

156. I wanted to start other classes but it was the only class I could start at the time. It turned out to be the most promising class because my major was geology. In this class, I found every single class I needed for the winter semester to get on my way to being a geologist.

Fall semester ended and winter semester was just beginning. I had to stop by college to find out my grade. I found that my GPA was a 4.0 from my counselor. Well now onto the bad news. I found out today from my counselor that there has now been some mix-up with the spring registration date. And unless my counselor, Mr. Rick, can fix it, I may not be able to attend spring semester for some major upcoming connecting classes.

The DSP&S told me about this mix-up so they sent me up to Mr. Martinez. I spoke to him and he said, "Everything was fine so he sent me back down to DSP&S to tell them that nothing was mixed up. All my classes were going to start and the date was fine to get my spring classes. So all I got was a big day of going upstairs and downstairs.

Well, I start my English 098 class tomorrow and hopefully it'll be a better day. On January 6, 2015, that day was not a good day. It was neither bad nor good. Sometime while I was asleep, I had a mild seizure due to stress over beginning a new semester. Now that means I have to try half a year of being seizure free starting on the 7th which is tomorrow. I was so close because I stared on January 1st, and I was almost one week without having a seizure

But with the starting of my class today and my mom nagging me in the morning about how I had to get up for school again gave me so much stress. It was piled on me. I don't see why my mom has to give me so much hell for trying to pursue a career in college now to help the family. Yet she has to praise my younger brother since he has a job and a broken truck.

Greg goes to work by taking a skateboard or a bicycle or maybe even asking for a ride from a friend. However, I wake up at 6am three days out of the week, take a bus to college, and work my butt off just to try and get passing grades. Education may not be may not be making me money right now, but once I get that through with school, I'll be making more money than Greg is or wants to make in his whole life. My family will be coming to me. Then who do you think will be putting down who.

The good news that happened today is now I have all the supplies for class and some lab partners to study with. I intend to get no less than an "A" this semester so I am going to be studying real hard. If my lab partners can't keep up, then that's on them. I intend to walk out with an "A" or "A+" and no less.

I wish I could change my Mom's way of thinking or even better yet, my family's thinking about how hard I work more than Greg. All I hear is Greg this, Greg that. But in other people's eyes, isn't it the hardest worker that should be left alone no matter of his disability. I may have a disability, I admit, but I do not ask my family for any pity, any sorrow, or any help. I'm going to college, and I'm helping myself alone.

Greg, on the other hand, is making money and he's begging for help. And then I hear from my family, leave Greg alone. Joseph, don't bother Greg when Greg takes all of his anger on the people that try and help him.

On January 7th, I got my first English assignment. School went well. I asked my lab professor to check the book that I'm writing on the side called _The Hardened Life of the Future Dr. Calkowski._ I also asked my professor to help me with some criticism to see if I'm doing things wrong or right. My lady, Jade, is helping me with everything. I could not be luckier nor do I think anyone else could be luckier with such a woman.

He said, "Just email it to me, and he would read it and give me some advice if I need any. Tonight I ran into an old friend named Victor who became Brian and Manny's stepfather. We spoke about the good old days with Brian and Manny also James and Jack's fights that they used to get into. I heard that Brian is going to college as well and is taking care of his kids along with his wife and mother and stepfather.

Manny, on the other hand, lost his job. He still has children, but Manny's children are being raised by his mother and his wife. Manny is looking real hard for a job for all of them so that he can take his wife and children away from his mom's place and start living on their own.

Jade helped me out tonight with my first assignment. I just may pass because of her. But her mother was upset that day, and wasn't in a very good mood. The next day, her mother gave Jade a very nice mother and daughter apology when they spoke.

School Stress

TODAY WAS NOT A VERY good day at college. The only good thing that happened was that I got credit on my homework. However, I missed one piece of homework to put in my binder so it never got done. Next, I started falling asleep in class, and then because of that, I got pulled aside for a talk by both professors and some counselor.

You see, the night before I tried to do my homework with Jade in Temple City and then needed to get home, eat and go to bed. However, by the time I got home from eating, it was 11p.m. Now by the time I got my clothes and everything ready for school the next day, and finally got to go to bed, it was after midnight. I had less than six hours of sleep then I knew I was screwed.

I knew I had to get some homework finished that night, but even on the way to Jade's, I fell asleep on the bus. And by the time I was trying to finish my homework, I was almost dead tired. I was just able to make a bus, but the stupid bus driver even though I rang the bus bell late, she took me onto an expressway.

I then had to walk five or six blocks back. I sat down and had to wait two hours. My eyes were opening and closing. When I finally got home, I fell like a tree into Greg's bed. My mom's yelling did not wake me up. I was DEAD. The next day no one heard about me until 9:30a.m. That day I had slept eleven hours. But I only got up to take my medication then I went back to bed and got two and a half hours more. It was thirteen or fourteen hours of sleep that day.

Once I got up, I found out that Jade was already in Madison to help me with more homework. You see, I had texted her in the morning but never answered her because I was asleep. Jade was pissed that I forgot so I got dressed and hurried over to Taco Bell where we completed some homework. I found out not one but two assignments are to be done by computer. I sure hope I can complete them all by tomorrow or else I'm screwed.

Today you would not believe it, and I don't believe today. Besides the date, luckily not Friday but Tuesday, it was a day of hell. I swear it was one thing after another. I felt like I was a voodoo doll and that someone was just pulling the strings or putting things in my way. For instance, at Milestone it all started.

An assignment totally said the opposite of what to do or needed to be done. So they marked a zero for it. But I had a talk with the Dean of Milestone about something to do. Not to correct my grade but of one guy over there who seems to always be over my shoulder. Maybe's he's trying to have me drop the English 98, but I am no quitter. Next I came home and I wanted to write in here and the ink refills that I had in my school bag were gone. Just gone.

I was checking on the buses behind me all day and night. So I thought there would be enough ink to write with in this pen, but it was dry to the bone. So I started looking and I could not find one. I tried to call Bruce's on my cell phone. Then my cell phone says disconnected. By trying to call Bruce's, 411 gives me a number. It gave me a fax number.

I got today a bar salt and sugar holder for my bartending job, but then I look in my safe, and I see a book that can hold secret things sometimes. I look inside the book but only a napkin my mom gave me and USB cables were in there. So I remembered something that there was a larger one. I turned around to try and find it, and I find it. Then in it were three ink packages.

There was a phone number to Bruce's in a bag and close by was a bow tie and a cumber bun for bartending, and triple A batteries, three of them. Those I was looking for yesterday. What a screwed up day and a great day all in one. Now if only my professors can see how I misconstrued the work and reverse the grade that would be great.

Today's school was much better. Their dean had the head of the class department lay off me. Also the writing café is now being used by students because it's a clinic now to care about the student's studies. I guess my talk with the dean had the department start caring instead of treating students unfairly. I also got a seventy percent on the quiz which is just shy of a D, but a C.

If I had missed one more question, it would have been a D. How close, but I passed. Also, later on while I was on my way to Jade's, I had a damn seizure. Now I have to start over again, damn. Today, in the morning, Greg took me to school. I had just made class without a tardy or absence. Today was also so close to call to.

I was getting credit for things to be done in class. That was my English 98 class since I'm looking to pass and move onto English 99 in the spring semester. So far my attendance and grades are passing. If I can just keep it up, I should pass no problem. But besides Milestone, I have a dying mom, a girlfriend with cancer and looking for a place to live for Jade and me by my college, Milestone.

This is a lot of stress on me. While Greg is working, I'm doing homework. Then I need to get home by bus and go to sleep, and it may get worse in the spring semester because I'll have possibly four classes, English 99, Math 29, Art History, and a computer class if I can get in.

Today not only was I going to do my homework with Jade, but I found out some great news from her. Jade was told that her cancer was gone. Just two more chemo treatments to make sure it stays away. Then every few months to go for small check-ups. It was also our anniversary today when Jade found out.

We really celebrated that night. I took Jade to Coco's for dinner, and I'm not too sure if her mother was home that night because if she were, then I would have definitely invited her for dinner.

The book I was reading was great. I also did some data dumping tonight. Today, after doing the rest of my data dumping, I had turned in my blackboard assignment over the computer at Jade's home. This time I knew how to turn it in and complete the blackboard assignment. This time I won't get no C. I'll get much better for the extra studying.

Tonight, Jade spent the night over at my mom's place. You see, we were working on my first book. I'm now only chapters away from my first volume of my book which I call The Hardened Life of, the Future Dr. Joseph C. Calkowski Volume 1. Volume 2 is going to be called The College Years of the Future Dr. Joseph C. Calkowski. Once volume 2 is done, it will be one book maybe a movie one day or maybe I will make a volume 3. I just don't know yet.

But what I do know, is that my life as you can see, is just like one big movie. So I would not doubt that one day some director would probably take all the volumes, all my journals, and all my adventures and turn it into one big movie.

It was the day before school and my mama tells me about having Alzheimer's, an illness she just found out about that's in the progressive stages. I can't believe it the day before school again and this had to be given to me. It's enough that my mama's dying, but now, she may forget us all before she does die.

Well today is finally it, midterm day. I've been studying, reading, reading and studying with and without Jade's help. But mostly with Jade's help. Now is the big day. I'm a little bit nervous, but I guess it's only natural. But if I don't get seventy percent or better, I don't know how I'll feel because they only give me two chances. I really want to pass on my first try.

There's not a second chance because a second chance will hold me back. Also if I do take the class a second time and I fail, I will have to go to another city college to pass, and I don't drive. We'll see how today goes. Well today went from worried to relax and happy. I passed my midterm with a seventy three percent which is a C-, but I am checking to see the questions I missed because a lot of the questions I found to be easy.

However, in the last weeks quiz, I got a D, almost an F so now I'm questioning both tests. Now if I did earn those grades, I'm not complaining for now I'm at 800 points which is a B student. I'm not complaining because even if the scores were right, I'm still moving onto English 99. Today I also heard from my love Jade on her second day of chemo.

Today they gave her morphine for pain because they couldn't find her veins, and it was very painful. Today, unlike yesterday they made her cry by poking her for hours. My lady with her last treatments of chemo for the cancer, she had another worry. However, one worry is about to be lifted in February around the start of my spring semester, thank God.

The only thing about spring that's coming at me is college for six days a week. I'm calling this upcoming part in my life the dragon facing off the dragon. You see, I was born the year of the dragon in 1976 and my mother in 1940. But why I call it that, is not because my mother, but because I'm going to have a lot to face off against and endure such as school six days a week, and my mother's health.

That's a lot when both your brothers can't help. Greg works as a dishwasher hard and late. Henry has the hardest job. He's a father with a second baby on the way. It's due in August around his birthday. So that leaves me trying to do my homework because my mother boyfriend drives a cab until four or five a.m. the morning.

My hard life just got harder. Oh my mother's birthday was this past Sunday the twenty fifth, and it did not go well at all. It was probably because the day before I went to my sister's to see if she could help get Greg working at home cleaning after himself so mom won't stress.

It turned to hell when she suggested a schedule and Greg now won't go buy it. Maybe sometimes but not always. Now what really got to me was Victoria and mom are saying to leave Greg alone. Poor Greg, he has to work as a dishwasher, poor Greg needs to sleep. When what about Joseph. I'm writing a book that now will be published and going to college to become a geologist and I have to get up at 6a.m. and take it to the max three days a week. Now it will be six days.

Where's poor hardworking Joseph's life who is working for a career, and Joseph's sleep. I don't need sleep to get my associates degree. Then to move onto a four college. You do not call that hard work, and you don't need sleep? Comparing a dishwasher's life than to a man who is trying to make a career and get his PhD in Geology.

Having your own mother and sister saying that's doing nothing is an insult. Spring semester is hardly working out, and I thought it would. First, I get an English 99 professor from hell so then I changed to a different professor. This one turned out to be great. Her class matched perfectly with my math class on Friday's and Saturday's. Then I had on Tuesday's and Thursday's Art History.

Anyways, like I said, I thought things would be an easy ride and that nothing would go wrong. But like my father used to always say, "Don't count your chickens before they're hatched."

You see, the English homework and the math homework started piling on. So even with Jade's help, we would only be able to do the math homework and not concentrate on the English. By the time the math homework was done, I could not go about doing any reading assignments let alone writing assignments. It would already be passed time to go to bed.

It would be about 12 or 12:30 in the morning, and I needed to get up at 6am just to catch the bus at 7. I would always be getting a lot of Math and English homework to turn in the following Friday and Saturday. So by the time that I would try and catch up in English, it would already be the next Friday and Saturday with another assignment due in English and math.

So with all the stress and the hours of losing sleep, I would fall asleep on the buses and even in class. A couple of times I had a seizure at home and could not make it to class, and a couple of times I would work so damn hard until about 2 in the morning that I would not even be able to go to school.

By late March, my English professor said she would give me an F if I did not pick up the slack. So I had no other choice but to try harder and that just caused more sleepless nights and more seizures. Finally, I withdrew from English 99 and decided that I would probably take it next semester.

I started to have Math and just my Art History. But unfortunately, my mom and brother are getting in the way of my sleeping. Since Greg works sometimes until late hours in the morning, my mom screams and yells about Greg not bringing her dinner or coming straight home from work.

See sometimes Greg will get off work earlier than other times from different jobs, and he would go straight to his friends. When that happens, there would be nothing but bloody hell all over the house from my mom screaming and yelling. She would scream things like see he forgot me, and he does this to me all the time. I wish I were dead. Why God did you give me such irresponsible children?

Then that's when I would step in and say, "Did you just call me irresponsible?" And then I say to her, "Four days a week I have to do homework. I get very little sleep all because you want me to do Greg's chores, but yet I still do Greg's damn chores whether they be dishes or taking out the damn garbage."

And then later, I have to go back to doing my homework. I say, "Mom, by the time that I'm through with Greg's chores then done with my homework, I have to go to bed." In fact, it's past time to go to bed. I keep telling my mother that I'm trying to get a damn career here and all Greg is doing is stupid side jobs and sometimes working a retirement home.

And you're calling me irresponsible? So finally my mom wised up a little bit. But now, she screams and yells at me saying, "It's time to go to bed for school. I keep telling her that I'm sorry, but I'm still doing homework. So now it's my mom screaming that's keeping me up, and it's also about me coming home late from trying to do homework.

I had gotten a real lecture from my Art History today about falling asleep in class. My professor asked, "You want to tell me all about it, Joseph? Why are you falling asleep during my lectures? Professor, what can I say? I'm having difficulty with my mother, my brother, and my mom screaming because my younger brother isn't home from work yet.

Then usually by the time that I get done with my homework and get ready for bed, it's already past midnight. And in order to catch the bus, I have to wake up at 7a.m. Professor, my home is hell. I said, "Now if my mom were dead, I'd be able to pass this course. If I lived in my own apartment, I'd be able to pass this course. If my younger brother were not getting my mom so angry to the wee hours in the morning, I'd be able to pass this course. They don't care about my education.

All they care about is money. They don't care if I get sick in my sleep trying to further my education by getting some rest. Sometimes my brother may have to get up around the same time I do at 5a.m. because he has a job at about 6a.m. And always the night before what do I hear from my mother but, "Joseph you keep quiet. Greg is sleeping for work in the morning. There are times then I want to just raise hell with my mother all because she would remain quiet for Greg, but she raises hell for me when Greg is late.

This is my college life so far. I'm trying to find a place to live all because I know that there is no way I will get my Associates degree at the time I'm supposed to receive it by living with my family. But then again, I'm trying to hack it living with my family because I receive almost a thousand dollars a month in social security. If I were to move out, I could kiss all of that goodbye. It would be different if I had a job.

This is one of the reasons that I'm writing these books because my life is one big dramatic story. My younger brother even says, "Quit bringing so much drama into the house." Well, he and my mom are the drama. So by staying in the house of hell, I'm able to save almost a grand each month. So hopefully my books will be a huge success. Then when they want money, which is all they care about, I can just tell them to go back to their house of hell and let me relax in my house of heaven.

Getting to my Complications of my Friends and Loved Ones

T HERE WERE A FEW THINGS that did happen in February. On Valentine's Day, everything started out great being Valentine's day. There were gifts that were going to be exchanged and so were hugs and kisses. But then around the afternoon, I'm not even sure how it all started or even who started it though. There was an argument that started between Jade and I. It went back and forth word after word. My mom tried to have us stop, but before we did, bang. Jade just could not take it anymore, and said I'm out of here.

So I just said, "Fine." I still tried to give Jade her chocolates, but she said keep them. I don't want anything from you, Joseph. Jade left then. You know how sometimes people say things in anger but then try to take things back. Well, that's Jade. I'd broken up with her so many times for almost three years that I could not take her anymore. What I could not take was her 1 to 10 anger anymore. Especially that Irish anger.

In my opinion, her anger was the worst at that time. So Jade tried to come back to say she was sorry, but I had warned her that if she got angry, I would break up with her. I decided that we would only be able to remain friends so that's just what we are now. Jade helps me out when I need her help with homework, and I help Jade out when she gets down about things.

So far our social life has been an up and down journey. She has had her dates, and I have had my chats online. Well no dates, just heart breaks. I know, how can you have heart breaks online, but some women can make you feel that serious. But before you know it, the game starts.

I was serious, but now I changed my mind. That's why now I let it be known to women that if they are going to change their minds in the future, just move on.

However, by doing that, I've gotten to know only some serious women. But online recently, I was messed with. My whole profile made me look like a sex pig. At first, I accused Jade, but she swore on a stack of bibles that it was not her. So it remains a mystery. If I did not write some gross things about myself and Jade couldn't have, Who did?

I met a woman in college who became a friend. I gave her my number but did not hear from her for a couple of weeks. Her name was Julia. Anyway, one night she texted me all kinds of love talk making it sound like I stood a chance with her. She calls me in a voicemail and says, "She's my girl.

Then when we meet. Julia, tells me we cannot be together because we're from two different worlds she says. She was from a different background, and I'm an American. She says she wants to marry one day an American but not me because we do not know each other well. So I say, "Let's get to know each other."

Julia just said, "No." She played me a damn fool. However, there is someone online named Cynthia who likes me. We have a lot in common. We've spoken online but not dated yet. Jade still cares about me, and we remain friends.

I also sometime back in February had a dream about the family because I can read people's eyes. And in March sometime this month, we will be celebrating Greg's birthday. And Henry our older brother came, and I asked him about his upcoming baby. He was not even able to look me in the eyes. He just looked out towards the door. His heart was beating faster than he was talking.

Henry told me not to talk to his wife, Helena, about this. Henry said, "The home pregnancy test was inaccurate." The reason I didn't believe the test was wrong was because there was one thing he forgot that they mentioned at Christmas time. That was that they were able to see a child growing soo she was pregnant. I just don't know about why he would lie about it. I sure hope nothing happened to their baby. Henry lied to me, but he did not lie very good.

Something is wrong. I wish my brother would really be honest with me because I'd rather Henry be honest than having him lie to his own brother. I love both my brothers very much even though they can hurt me or say things that'll hurt me.

Today was really bad. It is the Thursday before Easter 2015. My mom had written chores for Greg and me to do. Greg started acting real weird. My mom was asking each of us to help. She said because Easter's right around the corner and our brother Henry, our sister-n-law, Helena, and our nephew, Augustin are supposed to be coming on Easter.

Anyway, my mom was asking Greg where he was going, and Greg just stayed to himself. That's just Greg being Greg. Finally, Greg's temper got so bad that he went up to our mother and an inch from her face he yelled and said, "I'm going into the fucking backyard to get the fucking lawn mower so I could cut the fucking front lawn. Is there anything else you want to know you fucking retard?"

I then said, "Greg you don't talk to your mother that way. Then Greg said, "You too. You God damn sons of bitches."

Our mom started crying and saying, "that's my son?" See this is going to be my Easter in tears. I wanted to beat Greg's ass so bad, but a long time ago, I swore I would never lay a hand on any of my brothers unless absolutely necessary.

So I got a hold of our sister Victoria by texting her, and Victoria was not much help. Basically she said, "You texted me three times. I'm at work. Do you know what three texts at work could do to me? And don't call Greg my angel." I was simply implying and telling her that because she gives Greg a lot more credit than she does to my mother or me.

She's even told us before just to leave Greg alone because he's under a lot of stress from work. Now what Victoria don't know or realize is that Greg takes a lot of hell out on our mother even me sometimes. Greg is a very abusive son and brother to live with and Victoria just sees him like the hardest working one in the family.

She doesn't believe that Greg drinks just like our step brother did. And Victoria once said when we were kids, "Never try and turn out like your brother, Joshua." You see, Joshua was a drunk, and Greg is on his way to becoming one. And all Victoria is will you leave Greg alone. He's thirty seven years old. He's old enough to drink.

She does not believe one word I say. I could talk to Victoria until I'm blue in the face that Greg is no good, and she would not believe me. Anyway Greg's friend, Mike, came knocking on the door, and I told him that Greg needed to stay because we have chores and I need him here. All Mike had to say was, "I'm here to collect Greg."

I said, "Excuse me." He then said, "You're not his father, Joseph." I said, "But I'm his older brother, and I need him here. Our mother needs him here." Finally he says, "Well I need him for a job." I said, "Can't you wait? You're his friend. Can't you come back in a little bit, after we're done?" He then says, "No, I need him now because I paid him in advance."

I said, "Well then, he's going to have to pay you back because we have some chores that need to be done." And then he says again, "you cannot control you brother, Joseph. He's thirty seven years old."

Greg then tried walking away. I was trying to talk to him and talking to him didn't seem to help. I said to him, "Greg can you please stop? Mom needs us." Greg would not stop so I tried to explain that mom was crying because it's near Easter, and I need his help. Why can't you just give Mike an excuse and that you need to help your brother and mother for just a little bit? Then I can help you, Mike.

Greg resisted. So I tried nicely to talk face to face with my younger brother because his back was towards me. I said, "I'm not going to hurt you." He said, "Get your hands off me." I said again, "I'm not going to hurt you. I just want to talk to you." My hands were on the straps of is backpack and on his shoulder. I tried to turn him around. Then Greg took a swing at me, and he hit me in the head.

I took that punch because I did not want to hurt my brother. You see, I taught Greg everything about fighting in martial arts, wrestling, boxing, everything. There's an old saying. The master can beat the student, but the student can never take the master. That's why I took the punch. I took many swings but was just socking his punches away by kind of blocking.

By doing that, I was breaking open his five closed fist. And I kept telling Greg, "Stop it, Greg stop it." One of his swings though hit me lightly in the testicles so I basically didn't want this anymore. I said, "I'm sick and tired of playing around with you." I grabbed Greg and took him into an Indian wrestling hold. A hold known to some masters. It gets your opponent or enemy, however you want to word it, from doing anything, any punches, or any kicks.

But I could not believe Greg still was still wanting to takes punches at me. And I said, "Greg, knock it off." Finally, Mike said, "Yes, Greg, knock it off." But when Greg was taking swings before I got him into this hold, there was one time where Greg tried to take a swing at me. When I socked away his five closed fist away, his face went into my five closed fist.

Greg did not obey the first rule of fighting that I taught him. Never attack in anger because you're sure to lose every time. I did not want to hit my brother in his head at all, but unfortunately, it hit him hard. Greg was very, very dazed and confused. Mostly because my punches would be like being hit head on by a coal train. My punches are very hard and very deadly.

I know and was taught from all my masters' three death moves. They taught me that because they knew I would never use them unless I was in severe danger to death. Also that I would never teach these moves to anyone else because hardly in the world you could you find someone that would be worthy of learning these moves without actually using them.

That's why thank God, I have never had to use them nor teach anyone. That night I felt so bad that I hit my brother and felt that I was a bad master as well as brother. My mom did not help at all either. I had just spent money riding around on buses, stopping and thinking from place to place. I was thinking that I just need to get out of my family's home.

If anything like that happens again, I could probably go to jail. The police came that day and they told me so. They told me that everything I had done was against the law even when my brother had attacked our mother by putting his hand on her throat and almost choking her a little a while back.

I asked, "Why would I be in trouble for that?" These stupid beginner cops said, "Because I did not try to stop my younger brother." How can you try and stop something when you don't even know that's it's going to happen? Greg has a temper that is uncontrollable. They called it battery for trying just to talk to my brother about our chores. They said, "when you put your hands on his backpack straps and just say, Greg, or my brother, can we please talk?" It's called battery

One of the officers said, "If you were my older brother and you put your hand on my shoulder, I would have just turned around and just taken you down." So you can see why I left that night. Everything was a nuthouse. The cops and my mother were talking trash to me. She said to the cops, "It's not my home that it's Greg's." Greg cannot be arrested.

If you're going to arrest anyone, it has to be Joseph. That Joseph starts everything. He has the temper and that Greg has no temper. So I left, but I ended up coming back that night because my mother said things were going to change. But the next day came, and things were getting worse. There was no change. There was nothing. I even found out that day that Greg was needed more than I, and my mother denied talking any of that trash to the cops.

The next day I ran into the Perez sisters on my way meeting with Jade. I then found out some terrible news. An old friend of mine that I've known since grade school had died due to a heart attack from drinking and smoking. His name was Elias. Elias and I used to fight, but we would fight just to spite each other. You know to fight to see who was the strongest or who was the coolest in fighting.

He had a twin brother named Sam. I believe they were both Arabic. They also had a sister. I can't really remember her name. but from what I heard, his twin brother did something really great because of his death. He became a new born Christian.

I also found out that a lot of my classmates of Madison High either moved far away, died, has gotten married, and have children now but are very poor because they do not have the money or the funds to raise children. Let's just say this. My old friends or my old classmates of high school made some really bad choices after high school. I did not want to show any emotion in front of the Perez sisters but that night I really took Elias's death bad.

That night I just cried because he was a great friend, and I hope to see him one day in heaven. Because I believe he still owes me a rematch.

The next day was Good Friday. Now I don't know if you believe in angels coming just at the right moment, just at the right time but I believe one did on Good Friday.

You see, Jade who I was just thinking about just as a friend at the time. I was having a discussion between my mother and I. I felt that Jade was on my mother's side, and my mother was just trashing me a little. I don't even remember how it started or what it was even about. All I know is that I was really thinking in my mind Jade needs to go.

However, just before I could do anything or say anything, I heard some knocks at the door. It seems that Greg had a friend that lived across the street who was part Polish. She was asking for Greg's help but Greg was gone. He was working that day somewhere. Anyways, we started talking. It was about her moving and moving because she did not have a roommate to share the rent with across the street.

So I called to Jade to come outside and talk to this woman about a place for rent. My mother and this friend of Greg's and Jade all started talking. At first they were talking trash about guys. She was mentioning how the day before her boyfriend talked some trash to her at the Arcadia In N Out and all she did was bust him in his nose. He just said over and over while holding his nose, "Okay I'm sorry, I'm sorry."

She was saying that you got to put men in their place. I then stepped in and said, "Oh, the usual talk between women." She started mentioning to me how long have you two been together? We were afraid to say or I was afraid to say that we were together. She's all saying, "Well, this is your girlfriend isn't it? I didn't really want to let her know that Jade and I were broken up.

But then she just goes it's a yes or no question. Is this or is this not your woman, and how long have you been together? I told her that we had broken up on Valentine's Day. She caught me in a lie because I had said a few minutes before that Jade was my girlfriend. It was mostly because my mother said that Jade was my girlfriend.

I then tried to explain things. I explained how Jade wasn't my girlfriend. But then every single complaint I had about Jade, every single thing I had to say, she had an answer for. Something like an angel would have done or do to stand up for Jade. Jade was not saying anything, but just listening. She was not even disputing.

This womand says, "See this woman really loves you. If she did not really love you, wouldn't she be arguing with you right now. She is letting you do all the talking, and so, she's nine years older than you. Soon someone may pick up Jade for being very beautiful or you after your education. In your upcoming life, you won't find another woman like Jade, and you would be very devastated if you actually let this woman go and slip right through your fingers.

I told her that she can't even have children, and I want children of my own. She first asked Jade, "You do have a uterus still don't you? And Jade exclaimed, "Yes." She said then, "Well, of course you can have children. There is a thing called artificial insemination." She described it like this. It's where the doctor takes my sperm and cleans it. Then he takes her eggs cleans her eggs so that nothing from our family's genes could transfer to the child.

She tried to speak about adoption. I even thought that I had her there because I checked on adoption, and when you adopt, you have to be eligible to adopt. She spoke of some sort of friends of hers that were supposedly in some sort of way or another that had adopted. So Jade and I decided to get back together and just before Easter. It was on Good Friday. Isn't that ironic because Good Friday in the Catholic religion is the night that Jesus died for us.

On that Saturday, I had an argument with my mother so I got my things together and I went over to Jade's. I was over at Jade's for just a little bit. Then I called up our friend, Juan, and he took me over into the city of San Gabriel to a motel called the New Century Inn. I spent the night there and then spent Easter with Jade's family.

At Easter it also happened to be her uncle Ken's birthday. Once everybody had left, and it was just me there, I called up my mother. She said, "Everything was going to be different and everything was going to change like she usually does. But I felt like such a fool because after I left to go home with Juan, the next day came and everything basically went back to hell.

I asked my mom why did she start up again. I said, "You told me that everything was going to change, andnd she just said, "How can things change?" I said to her, "So I spent nearly two hundred dollars going over there and then coming back because I believed you, and you lied to me? She said, "I didn't lie to you but how can things change?"

My mother's nothing but a hypocrite because I never know when she's lying or telling the truth. She usually lies just to try and make it sound like the truth. That's why I call my mom a hypocrite. That night Greg came home, and I told him that karma is going to hit him hard. He said, "If I'm guilty of anything, then I guess it will."

My mom told me that night that since she did not have enough money to help pay for the cab fare, or help pay to get me home and that if I paid for everything to get myself home, Greg would pay me back. Yet my mom said then, "Where's Greg going to get that money that night. He has no money." She just said everything to get me home to try and not make me leave again.

I've been arguing with my mother for a couple of days now. On Wednesday, Jade came to help me with my book again. Jade's been a sweetheart. I guess my friend, Tara, a psychic advisor, was right in finding the woman that I was going to spend the rest of my life with.

On Thursday, I called up Jade and asked her to go with me to the Mc Diner basically because I cannot take my mother's lying anymore. I needed to concentrate on my book and a lot of other things, and how could I concentrate on all that stuff with my mother's yelling day and night, night and day.

So I stayed one night at the motel, and I had a dance with a cockroach from hell, but he learned his lesson. Never to mess around with a Polish man. I reported this incident to the front desk, and they started saying, "Well, why didn't you report this last night." I kept telling them I was asleep. I didn't find out about this until I woke up. They said, "Why didn't you report it then."

I said, "Now look. You can either give me a free night stay or refund my money or I go straight to the health and safety code department. They said, "Well if that's what you got to do." So I got a hold of San Gabriel City Hall code enforcement. They got back to me the very same day and left a message for me saying, "They were going to do an investigation. I just needed to get back to them." They left me the health department's number as well. So we'll see who has the last laugh now.

Friday night when Elvis came home, my mom's boyfriend, he said things and trashed my mom all over the place. He said, "If your mom's going to fucking die, let her fucking die. I said, "You're talking about my mom right there." I wanted to hurt him so bad, but the police told me that if there's going to be any disputes, to call them first.

So I basically left the room. I'm just leaving it to Karma now. Karma pretty much took care of my younger brother. For some reason, he has a flat tire. So I'm hoping that karma will hit Elvis. Even though he trashed my mom all over the place, she's still defending him, her babe.

I heard them have an argument this morning about how he wishes he could take away all the favors he's done for me back. He said, "Why don't you just stop doing favors for him?" Well, in his own words, why don't you just stop doing fucking favors for him. That's just like his favorite word.

I got into an argument with my mom after Elvis left, and I told her that I read up on my seizures and my seizures are not epilepsy. They're psychologically triggered by stress, not that I don't need medication. I told her that I hold her and my father personally responsible for stressing me out all the years that I was growing up with them because it was torcher growing up with them.

There was hardly a night that they would not fight about something whether it be stupid or personal. They would still fight. I had to be in the next room sleeping with my sister listening to all their arguing, and sure enough, I would end up having a seizure in the morning.

Sometimes I could not go to school. Sometimes I would take the stress with me to school and then the kids would start poking fun at me pretending they would be having a seizure.

I'd become so fragile that the little bit of stress would trigger a five to ten minute seizure, and my mom just denied everything today saying it wasn't her fault. It wasn't your father's fault. What arguments are you talking about? She told me I was talking lies, and I was crazy. She was saying all this in front of my girlfriend, Jade.

I told her that I had gone five and a half months once without a seizure because I was out of her home and living with Jade. All I had and needed was just her out of my face and Jade's love. My mom's all saying that you're lying and that can't be true. You're father and I did not cause your seizures from any stress and that it was just brought on. I told her seizures cannot be just brought on. It needs to be triggered by something.

Apparently just before he died my father and my mother went out to eat. He said to my mother, "I know that I am dying, but when I die, at least I'll be free from that son of a bitch, Joseph." You don't know how much that hurt me. It felt like my mother tore out my heart and just spat on it. I don't know how I could ever forgive my mom. I'm figuring now that I don't have a mom and I can never forgive her for this not even in death. I could forgive even if she asks for forgiveness before she dies. Because right now, I have no mother, and she has no son. I have to live with the truth now of how my father felt towards me and what he had told her just before he died about me.

I thought for about it for nearly twenty four years now that my father's last words to me in this world were I love you, Joseph. Basically, I got a hug good bye when I was in the hospital getting some help. Today, however, my mom told me the truth of what his last words were about me. I will have to live with that the rest of my life.

Jade even called her up and said, "Renia, how could you say that to Joseph?" She started telling Jade, she was sorry, but she was just angry at the time. She started crying and said how much she loves me and wants me back. She is really hurting over this now. I just want to get the hell out of there and buy some tickets on the 15th then have Jade and I hit the road.

You know I just want to take some trains, take some buses, and just go wherever the road takes us. Just like that one song we'll be just like dust in the wind. But as far as tonight, I don't know where I'm going to go. And as you can see, this is some of the stuff that I have to deal with when I really want to go to college but can't with a mother like her.

I don't know what's going to happen but I still want to go to college for I need to go to college to shell out all those people; all those people that I used to call family out of my life. I want to show them all that I went to school; I graduated from college; I transferred to a university, and I graduated from a university.

It's a long road of hope, but I know that with Jade's help, and me keeping an optimistic appraisal of the situations that co I can defeat any challenge that may come ahead. I finally bought some stock. I also made a joint account with Jade because of how much I trust her. She's my lady, and I love my Jade very much.

Now as far as my family goes, same old hell going on. My family is impossible. They do not believe in family time. They do not believe in family love. They do not believe in family happiness. What their vision of family is nothing but the love of the money and doing the blame game with the IOU's.

I've tried. I believe I wrote about this before not too sure, but I tried to get the hell out of the house. I tried to get away from this family environment because around them I definitely get seizures. It's not the kind of environment that My family says it's ridiculous. That I'm totally in a stress free home, and that they're not doing anything to me. Also they said it's just school stressing me out. Now how can that be when I'm on spring break. There's no homework, no teachers, and no counselors. It's just me and them. The people that I'm supposed to call my family.

My mother lies to me just to get me back home when I do leave. It's not to say that any mother who would love their child would do anything, however, my mother makes all these promises of change in the home. It never happens though. She says that things are going to be different.

I try and tell my mom of how many neurologists have declared my seizures just psychologically brought on. In other words, brought on by stress. She says, "There will be no more stress in the home, no fights, and no arguments. And yet, my brother is now leaving for days at a time instead of just one day at a time. I get stuck with my mother yelling at me. She yells at me about what Greg should be doing.

All this interferes now with mine and Jade's life. If I say I'm going to meet Jade, my mother has a fit about it. I'm in a house that is already looking like trash because my mother is a hoarder. "She says, I'm the one that makes a real mess." Ever since my siblings and I were little, she saves every single thing. To her it was so-called special.

There were only a few times that I can remember my father, my mother, and my siblings actually being able to eat around that table. Now the whole dining room has junk everywhere even all around that table. In the thirty nine years of my life, my mother never once thought of getting a yard sale together and actually selling some of that stuff.

When my father was alive, he used to always argue with her about hoarding anything and everything. But she never took care of it because everything was so special that she didn't want to get rid of it. We're talking cups, baby clothes, clothes that my siblings and I grew up in and don't even fit in anymore.

She never looks through it. All she does is keep on living the same old life and loves her boyfriend. Elvis, gets up in the morning and tries to wash clothes day after day after freakin day. I've tried to talk her into yard sales because I have some things that I want to get rid of. However, all she says is, "Wait and let me go through this stuff."

After talking to her like this for about ten years, I would think that she would get a clue. It seems though that the only time that we will ever be able to have a yard sale is when our mother is gone. I hate to say that but she won't budge. She won't look through things because everything to her is way too special.

Now Jade and I have been talking about marriage for quite some time now. In June, it's going to be three years together. I sure hope that her family will accept me and help Jade and myself with the wedding because we don't have the money right now. The groom is supposd to pay for the ring and her family pays for the rehearsal dinner the night before the wedding, I believe.

I highly doubt my family will want me getting married at all just because they would have to put in a penny to help make both Jade and I happy. But knowing Jade's family, they like me a lot much better than her ex-husband. So I believe her family would do anything just to make us happy. My mother gets into our business a lot.

Jade's mom just stays out of the way. She mostly keeps to herself and to her grandchildren. I told my mother the other day that once this book comes out who do you think will be coming to who for money? My mother just complained and fought with my father about becoming free and just letting her work as in getting a job.

Now my father's dead and has been for almost twenty four years. Once she got her boyfriend, Elvis, she started I'd say to treat Elvis a little bit like she treated my father. She would say to my father you know give me a little bit of money here, give me a little bit of money there. But Elvis really stands up to my mother because he lets her know where his money needs to go.

For instance, his money needs to go to pay for the lease on his cab. Also Elvis has been kind enough to help pay property taxes because Greg hardly gets enough money in his side jobs to cover hardly any of the property taxes. Now we're four thousand dollars in debt with back taxes that are due by the end of June this year 2015.

That's why, I said to my mother, "Who do you think is going to be coming to who once I get money off this book." I just don't get it. When I started this project, my mother spoke to me about writing her own life story because my mother was born during the start of WWII.

In her mind, she has a whole book of memories being born during the start of WWII and through her life until the present. My mother's life could actually make a great movie and a very great novel. It would go beyond the minimum words and pages of a novel. Anytime I ask my mom, "When are you going to get to it?" My mother says the most ridiculous thing. She says, "I need sometime alone when my brother and I aren't even around during the day so I can think about what I want to say."

My brother's is off at work, my mother's boyfriend, Elvis, he's off at work, and I'm at either school or out of school. After school, I go straight to work on my writing. My mother is all alone. If I were her, I'd have all the time to write several books. Yet, she complains that she does not have enough time and that we should leave her alone.

I've given her a tape recorder so she could record her thoughts and that way I could get Jade to type down her thoughts for her book. What does she do though, she's working herself into her grave by doing laundry. This is the most ridiculous thing that's happening now. She has even more time because she can't even do laundry like she wants to because the damn washer's broken.

She got a new one, however, the new one turned out to be a piece of crap. Greg has no time because he's working so much to get the warranty together. Then go to Sear's to get a better one.

I recently spoke to my mother, and she's saying that she may actually write her book. I explained to her that Elvis is gone during the day, Greg's gone during the day, and I'm gone during the day. I might be at school or even after school I go straight to work on my book.

I asked her "so where is everybody?" You're by yourself. You always say you want to have money. You have all the time in the world while we are gone. She mentioned something about that she doesn't have time because she has to clean up. I just said, "Mom, you do not have to clean up. And even if you do, you can still set sometime aside to work on your book."

I explained that the recorder that I gave to her has hours and hours and hours of recording for her to use. She thought that she should use a regular recorder. I said, "Mama, this recorder that I gave to you to use almost has, and this is true, almost has a million and a half hours. I looked at it myself."

When I told my mom, she asked me, "Do you think I'd really get paid?" I said, "Mama, you have a best-selling novel in your mind and another thing, mama, they could possibly turn your novel into a movie."

She said another negative thing which was, "I don't have time during the afternoon, but I could probably make sometime in the early morning." There's something about my mom I will never forget because of what she said. My mom said, "I need to get all these memories down before my Alzheimer's gets it first and erases all my memories." I said, 'Well, make that time. If you start working on this book, Jade and I will help you. So she said the only possible positive thing I heard which was, "Okay, Julian. I'll do it."

Now me, I'm an optimist so I'm going to keep an optimistic appraisal of the situation. I told her, "If you don't write this book, then you're going to lose out on a lot of money. Also you're going to lose out on a lot of publicity. It could be published not only out here, but your book could be published out in Poland too."

She said, "Poland too?' I said, "Of course. This book could be published anywhere. It's a great publishing company that I'm hooking you up with, and a lot of people want to know about WWII since a lot of medals of honor were given."

I recently ordered a coin and stamp collection that were made during WWII, and a hell of a lot of countries were in the WWII. I heard from my father, my mother, and also by watching so many WWII movies of presidents giving hundreds and hundreds of medals of honor away to so many brave soldiers. It was incredible to me. So many brave countries and so many brave souls makes you wonder why did the Germans do such horrible things.

THE OLD FEELINGS

The Old Friends

ITS VERY FUNNY HOW SOMETIMES when you're trying to concentrate on certain things and then all the sudden out pops another story of your childhood. On my way home today, I could not believe it. I ran into another old friend who I grew up with. I didn't really recognize him at first because my brother's friend had a beard, and the sun was kind of in the way. He hollered out, Joseph.

I turned around, and then he shouted, "Your name, Joseph?" I said, "Yes. "He said, "You recognize me, man? How you been?" I said to myself at first, who is this guy? I also said to myself I know, I know him because I can recognize half his face. So I went to the other side of the Coffee Bean and Tea Leaf because he was going through the drive thru.

I then said to him, "You know I recognize half the face because his beard is covering the other half man." He just laughed and said, "The beard yeah. It's me, Derrick. I used to live over on Olive around the corner from you."

I said, "Oh yeah, man. How you doing?" He said, "How you doing." I told him, "I'm halfway through a book that I was writing." Derrick and some friend of his asked, "What it was about."

I said, "It's about my life." They just said, "It's a good thing to write about." I accidentally scared the waitress that was waiting on him because she didn't see me at firs and I was by the drive thru window.

I said, "It's okay we grew up together." So I said, "You living back on Olive." He said, "No." He said, "I was living on Canyon but now I'm

70

hitting the freeway and we're headed to Arizona. I just need an expresso with a couple shots to keep me awake.

So I saw Derrick off, and we said our goodbyes. We were saying about how nice it was seeing each other, and another friend that I grew up with is now gone in my life.

Its sad how I'm seeing and hearing about my childhood friends and buddies either dying or just having a terrible life. It goes like that sometimes in life. Right now in my life, I'm trying to make something of myself by going back to college. d I got distracted by the memories of the good times and the bad. It's like a childhood phobia right now.

Only the phobia is just telling me to start saying goodbye to all the friends you knew and loved. I even ran into today a friend of mine named Westy and also another friend named Robert. I spoke to them for a bit. It seems Westy has a client that is doing him a favor by trying to find his older brother, Randy.

Randy was very close to his mother growing up, but I guess after she died, he felt he had nothing to lose in life. So he started down a wrong path and has been in and out of prison. I feel really bad for all my childhood friends because they're dropping like flies in my life. They're either too poor and having children or they're making bad decisions in their life, and those bad decisions are taking their life.

I just wish I could find all of them and then help them out especially this one friend that I had been searching for. I've been searching for him for years now. I hope he reads this book because I mentioned his name in the beginning. He was my friend, and he was my brother. His name again is Jaden Gordon. And Jaden, if you're reading this, please try and find me.

Anytime I try and find you, I find about eight to ten Jaden Gordon's. So please, I know you can remember me if I can remember you. I'm still in my city, Jaden on the same street, and I'll be waiting for you. Now, if anyone related to the Jaden Gordon that I'm talking about knows anything about my best friend and brother, please try and contact me too.

A SMALL MIRACLE

I T WAS SUNDAY NIGHT AND Jade suggested going to church. We
were walking from the Mc Diner, and we finally get to the church.
There were many children and teenagers out there. I found out that
most of them were coming back from a retreat and that most of them
were going to do their confirmation. But as usual, everyone carries a story
of a little miracle or something that they just cannot explain.

Some of those people carry them in secret or are brave enough to go
up to the altar, and in front of the whole church, explain what happened
or what they even experienced. Now as usual after the gospel was read,
the priest takes about five or ten minutes of explaining some things that
really happen in life or that even compares to the bible. Although they
still are present events.

The priest that night mentioned how when Pope Francis came out
of the Vatican one evening, someone questioned him with these words.
"Who do you think you are?" The priest mentioned because some people
out of the church and outside the Vatican hate us. He said, "Whether
you're a pope, a priest, a bishop or a cardinal some people still hate us.

Now Pope Francis, when he was faced with that question, he said to
someone, "I'm just a sinner with a God that loves me." Once I heard those
words, I felt something inside me a little calling of understanding as if I
knew those words all along and that I was going to have an assignment.
After he explained that, but before he stopped, he said, "There are some
teenagers who would like to express what they felt at that retreat."

There were about six to maybe eight teenagers, and all of them said
something, but there was only one of them that had true heart feelings

towards what she saw and said, and why she was doing all of this. She was the last speaker, and I say the best because of what she said really tuched my heart and that's when I felt my calling and knew what I had to do.

I knew I had to stop her tears, and I knew Jesus was going to help me because he wanted her tears stopped. I was in church next to a friend. His name was Bruce Medina. I went to school with his sister, Mary and his brothers, Herman and Sammey who later on in the Oak Tree called him Dangerous.

Anyway, Jade was sitting a few aisles up. I wasn't able to tell Jade what I was feeling, but I told her after church and she was very proud of what I had done. You see, when we were saying our profession of faith, I usually close my eyes when I say my prayers, but this time I saw and felt a touch from GOD.

My Godmother telephoned my mother after church. When I told her all this my Godmother said, "It was the Holy Spirit I saw and was feeling. I had no doubt because it made perfect sense because right after I saw that light, even though my eyelids were closed, I felt a joyous feeling that made me smile. So I left my aisle, and walked over to the girl. Her name was Sofia, and I told her I was very proud of her.

I also had told her that she had picked the perfect time to cry, but I also said, "There's a time for happiness and a time to cry. I said if you're going to cry, cry it all out because the family of yours that are departed, they don't want you crying. They want you to be happy because they're in a better place. I said, "I know what you're feeling because a lot of my family are departed."

I told her I hardly ever got to know any of my grandparents. They're all dead. I only have one parent left and that's my mother, and I don't know when she will die but when my father died. I gave him one gift. It was the last sunburst I ever made. When you need your departed family, they'll sometimes come in your dreams just to visit you.

I told her it takes a lot of guts to do what you did and go up there like you did and tell everyone the reasons behind why you did everything. I told her my name was Joseph, and take care Sophia. I'll keep you in my prayers. When I went back to my aisle, I felt another feeling, and it was coming from the cross I was wearing. You see, on the cross I was wearing, it said, "With God all things are possible."

I then felt that my task was not yet done because I was feeling my cross, and it felt like I did not need this cross anymore. I just needed to pass it on to someone to make them happy. So when we were giving each other peace, I first went to Jade and gave her a kiss. I said, "Peace be with you" as I usually do. I then held the cross in my hand and went over to Sophia again and I then said, "May the peace of the Lord be with you, Sophia."

She then asked me who I was. I then said, "I'm just like the father said. I'm a sinner with a God that loves me." And then she said, but what's your name again?" I said, "My name is, Joseph. I'm giving you this cross because this cross it says in it with God all things are possible. I want you to know that someday your family will prosper and grow and that you will never be alone. Wear this cross until one day you will feel that you will need to pass this cross on to maybe a son or a daughter or even someone that you feel will need it more than yourself. I said someone good once gave me this cross because they felt that I needed it and now I'm passing this cross to you because I feel you need it more than I.

And when I looked into her eyes, there was not one tear. She was very happy. So I said again, God bless you, Sophia and take care. I went back to my aisle and then it was closing time after the body and blood of Christ was given. The priest called up the people that were going to make their confirmation and that had been to the retreat. Sophia was one of them. She looked very happy up at the altar, and then when she turned around, I noticed that she was wearing the cross I had given her because I saw the silver cross sparkle like a star in the sky as if it was letting me know that my task was done. So I just looked up to heaven, and I just nodded with my head, yes, as if we did it, God.

I told this to my friend, Bruce just before I told this to my Love, Jade, and he said, "You mean the girl that was crying up there? I felt for her too. "Way to go, Joseph." After church, I started thinking about how I needed to complete my confirmation in order to marry my love, Jade. However, a coincidental thing happened. Bruce who had not completed his confirmation yet, was asking me if I would complete confirmation hiswith him.

So it was like God through my friend Sammy was letting me know that it's time to complete confirmation. I mean what are the chances that two friends who have known each other for so long have not yet completed both their confirmation. That had to have been a small miracle happening that night because I was needed for this young girl, Sophia to help stop her fears and God used me to help stop her tears.

Then right after mass had ended, God uses one of my best friends to give me a little encouragement or I would say a tap on the shoulder or even a little hint, or nudge. By telling me through God's own words you know, Joseph, you're a good man but what about your confirmation? You need to do it because how can you marry that woman you love?

My Mother's Confusion

I've spoken recently to my mother about writing her own book because my mother keeps letting her friends know and keeps telling all of us about her life. My mother, ever since I can remember her mentioning this, has always told us she was going to write a book about her life. And about how she was born during the beginning of WWII. And now sometimes, my father actually visits me in my dreams.

She said, "She would always find time to write. Now quite a while ago, she wanted to write really badly when I was taking my English 98 class. So I gave her a recorder and told her if you're going to write this book, mom, record your thoughts on it. Now here I am writing a book about my life and every single day that I mention to my mother can remind her that she has all the time in the world. She can set aside fifteen minutes, a half hour, I told her even an hour.

My mother is a stubborn Aquarius. She keeps saying, "Alright, I'll do it, but I need to do it on my time when I want to." I tell my mom I'll help invest in you mom by paying to get you all the help you need. I will get you a publisher that will edit your book and get it your book published and distribute it to market. All you need to do is just work on it, but it seems my mother is having some sort of confusion because she's telling me that she needs to do all the work around the house when there's hardly any work to be done.

I mean, I get up and make my bed, I take a shower, and I meet Jade to write this novel. She says, "I'm leaving her with all the work." She says that every day. She says that even when Greg has to go off to work that he's leaving her alone as well. We are both doing things to make money. I put aside with my darling, Jade, hours of writing.

My mother's just complaining that her washer is broken. My mother and younger brother are having a rough time with Sear's now because Sear's sold them a crappy washer. Now they want to get a different kind of washer but pay about three hundred dollars on top. However, Sear's and my brother are having words exchanged because he wants to get refunded, because for some reason, they won't really want the three hundred on top.

So now there's a big mess between my brother, my mother, and Sear's. Maybe the reason my mother says she has so much work when she really doesn't, and has a lot of time, is probably because of stress or it could be a combination of stress, anger, and confusion due to Sear's. I spoke to my mom last night, and I told her about writing her story would be a winning best seller.

I told her just about how much she could possibly get at the least and that was a very big amount for a story like hers. She said, "Oh my God. Well then I guess I better get on it. What the hell am I waiting for?"

Then today I woke up at about 8:30 in the morning. My mom woke up around ten or so. I was speaking with my love, Jade. We were talking about her brother's little princess, Sierra and her little niece who is about a year old.

She was saying hi to me over the phone. Sierra has these little nicknames for everyone because she's learning to talk. She calls her twin brothers Samby and Brandon, Dot-Dot for Brandon and Bit-Bit for Samby. I don't really know what she calls Jordan and Tyler her other two brothers. I guess neither does Jade, but I have a nickname actually. I have to now that Sierra calls me. One is Ju-Ju and this time she came very close to saying my name, but the other name is Julie-Ju.

We'll see what she calls everyone when Sierra turns two. But she is so beautiful and I would be honored to be her uncle once I marry my love, Jade.

There's another thing about my mother. Anytime I mention about marrying Jade, she always gives such a negative response. Sometimes she says, "Are you sure you're not going to break up again. You know if you marry her and you don't want to be with her anymore, it will be a divorce. Are you sure that's you're going to stay together, and are you sure you're going to stay in love?"

And like I keep telling my mother, of course, I love Jade. Without Jade I'm not whole. She's the other half of me. What I'm not, Jade is. I'm good with words and Jade's good with numbers. I'm good with names and faces, and Jade can point them out. What I mean by that is, if I asked Jade where is such and such person, Jade would show me.

Jade and I had a great kinship with both our fathers. But for some reason, we don't quite have a good kinship with our mothers. Both are fathers died and both our mothers are alive. Jade's great with typing and I'm more of the one finger typist. That's why this book and many others to come are being made by both Jade and I.

I dictate and Jade types. There's a strong opposite attraction to make whole and become one between both Jade and I. That's what makes our relationship strong and grow. However, my mother does not see it. When I call Jade over the phone at night, and then I say, "Good night, Love, my mother says "Oh boy or oh God." Anytime I try and tell Jade that I love her in some sort of way with words, my mother just thinks that it's ridiculous.

It really pisses me off as well as my love, Jade. Jade is very beautiful. She may come from a rough family, but then again, so did I. Also who doesn't come from a rough family. I can probably name so many friends of mine that has a rough family, but I'm not going to. The point I'm trying to make is my mother should be a little bit more supportive because she used to be.

Also when Jade comes over, my mother greets her with a kiss and tells me something different. My mother is a very strange woman to understand. That's probably why my father and her did not get along while I was growing up. But my mother told me the other night, that when they got married he was a very passionate man. I hope she started today on her book because I know once my book is done and I'm getting paid, she will want some of my money, but my books are between Jade and I fifty-fifty. So it's our money. Mine and Jade's

My mother is having her chance to become very wealthy, and all she say's every day is I have no time to write. I keep telling her that Jade will do the writing. You just need to speak into the microphone, and yet, she stil speaks of no time to do it. I spoke to her last night, and just like I figured, she did not touch the recorder.

She keeps making excuses, and it's pissing me off. I asked Greg last night how was the Sear's thing coming along? And he said, "It's coming along much better so there should be no stress amongst my mother and Sear's."

My life of seizures is going great now because I'm doing something that I want to do which is write my book with my love's help. With Jade's love and my mind, writing this book is taking my seizures away.

If any seizure comes along now, it would only be caused because of my mother and because of her stupid excuses of me not working hard. I told her that last night when she confronted me, and she just said, "You were just sitting on your ass with Jade all day long. You weren't doing anything."

I said mom, "I was dictating, and Jade was writing." She said, "Oh dictating – how many words? You probably just did a little bit and then started sitting on your asses." Mom, Jade wrote until she was totally exhausted because I dictated nearly two thousand words. Jade was getting very exhausted towards the end, and I asked her, "You don't call that work? I told her Elvis works, Greg works, and I work. I have more than half this book done. I'm turning it in on the first of June. It will have sixty thousand words or more."

I then asked her, "You don't call that a mind job? I work with Jade every day on this book. Tomorrow I'm probably going to be doing the same thing because I have a deadline that I promised my publisher. Do you know that if you don't start getting to work on this book, every single thing in your mind that we all need to know from your birth, from the war, from your life is going to go with you when you die."

All my mother had to say was, "Don't you think I know this, Joseph? I hollered at her and said, "Then get to work on your damn book because don't you think that when you die Alexander, your grandson, would want to know about his grandmother and what she was like, what her life was like, and what she experienced growing up."

I said, "Austin and Jackie, they don't even know their own grandmother's life, but I heard that they want to." She just said to me, "Oh, that's a bunch of bologna."

I tell you my mother does not know what she wants in life. She says one thing and does another. I don't think my mother will write this book that she keeps talking about until my book is published, and I start receiving money for all the hard work I put into this book.

My mother is all about the damn money, and it's always been about the damn money. You see, my mother, if it's not sweepstakes or the lottery, she's trying to get money from her son's. She always needs some sort of reason with life surrounding money.

I'm a little bit angry at my mom because last night I needed to go to bed early, or should I say as soon as possible, but Greg calls, and he said, "He would be home in a half hour."

My mom tells me Joseph, Greg's coming home in a half hour. I then mentioned that I have to be in bed. She said, "It's only a half hour."

After Greg gets home, I need you to lock up and shut the porch light off because Greg always forgets. I said, "Okay, mom." It was about 11:30, and Greg did not come home until 2a.m. My mom and I got all over Greg because he held up my sleep, and he said that all he needed was to grab some things and he'll be back in the morning. However, when he did call my mom, he said that he was going to be staying the night.

So then I got a little angry with my mom, but I'm more angry with Greg. My mom and I made an agreement that we need to get a hold of Victoria and Henry to have a family meeting about Greg's behavior and responsibility.

So today, I'm going to be sending Victoria a text. I don't like to stab my brothers in the back, but I need to let Victoria know so that she can take care of the problem.

That kind of stress and no sleep can give a writer, writer's block. And a writer, would just go on thinking and thinking and thinking. Greg needs to pay for this as well as other things. You see, Greg has been staying away from home. He comes and goes as he pleases anytime of the day or night. He doesn't realize the responsibility that he has and yet he still calls it his home.

Now how can someone say it's their home if they are running off and coming back and hardly spend any time there. I'm sure all parents would agree with this if their teenage runaways leave home and come back whenever they please and told the parents off. He says things such as fuck the both of you. I'm out of here. I could find a much better place to live because I don't need parents like you.

Whenever they feel that they need money or something you have, they say, "Mom, Dad, I'm home." For you parents out there, how do you think you would feel? You probably would feel the same way my mother does. You would feel very disrespected for one. They're trying to walk all over you. And no matter how old your children get. You would probably give in and give it to them.

You see, Greg is thirty seven now. He trashes our mother and does what he wants. He goes to work, comes home whenever he wants, trashes my mother again, gets some things and takes off all over again. In my mother's eyes and mine, Greg cannot call our house his home. He can call what he does visits, but we think he needs his own apartment.

Anyway Greg is a two timer to our mother because his friend's grandmother pays him to take care of their property, and he feels that he needs to get paid by his own damn mother in order to take care of it for her. This is just my assumption though. He also takes care of the lady's yard, cats, and dogs. She pays him and allows him to stay over there at times.

Greg still talks to this woman, Rachel, and feeds her more crap when we thought he had stopped. No such luck. She came over again and confronted my mother about what we do to Greg. Why is she even getting involved in this? She shouldn't be. All she is to him is an employer, but she acts more like some sort of lover.

I said to my mother, "Maybe she's giving Greg a little bit more than cash. You know, a little friend's with benefits. My mother said Greg would not be able to do that. I asked why not? I said, "She looks a little young even though she's a little older." My mother said, "She has a husband." I said that don't matter, mother. I said, "Does her husband live with her day to day?"

She told me that her husband goes out and works long periods at a time. I told her then why not. Because if he can sit around and talk shit about his own family with her while her husband is gone, it only takes a little time for sometime in the sack.

I told my mother that I heard a couple times from Greg that she lets him use her own bed to stay in at night so that he could take care of her yard and animals when she supposedly needs to go somewhere and take care of business. It's just like you said, mama. Greg gets to stay the night.

I said, "In her bed? Don't that sound a little personal? Would you let hired help sleep in your own bed if you did not have Elvis, Greg, or myself? Would you let it get that personal?" My mother said as usual, "Oh, hell no. I wouldn't let anyone in my home. What are you crazy?" I said, that's my point, mom.

I said, "Rachel is crazy. She may be over all the crap Greg talks, and a little crazy in love with Greg. You know, a little infatuation and needing a little romance while the husband's away. Who knows, she may even pay Greg for that. I know I would mom, if for instance, I had no one in my life, and I needed the money badly.

My mother thought and said to me that I was sick and disgusting and that I was crazy. My mom just doesn't understand. I guess she just doesn't understand the characteristics of a lonely middle-aged man that only has jobs here and there.

THE UPCOMING STRESS

THIS WEEK I'M GOING TO be going back to school again. My mom and younger brother stole my spring break. I do not regret though writing with my beautiful love, Jade. Jade has made my spring break awesome. However, I would have loved to go to the beach with Jade. Unfortunately, Jade has no car right now so now I had to just skip my whole break or in one word or another have a spring break of hell.

The only thing that made my spring break even come close to feeling like I was at the beach, you know happiness, a feeling that I was around my friends, the seagulls, was the family, the Baileys. But most of all Jade and I reunited back together by what we figured to be an angel because we got back together on Good Friday.

You see, we got back together on that day by a woman that was just looking for my brother. She told me exactly what I needed to hear about Jade, and she had an answer for every single argument I had about Jade. She didn't even know me. Afterwards, it seemed more that she came over to help us rather than needing my brother to help her move. Even her best friend was just like another me, and she was just like another Jade.

She knew what to say and when to say it, and all this happened on the day that Jesus died for us. We feel that Jesus felt that we should not be crying in tears over each other so he sent down an angel to dry our tears and bring us back together.

Recently I have spoken to my mother back and forth about the book and now there's a little miracle too. She finally started it. There are some kinks that she's working on with me, but I'm telling you after listening to at least the first chapter of her book, I have a lot more respect towards my mama. I also get on my younger brother anytime he disrespects her now because of all the hell I found out that my mother went through.

Since my mother was born during WWII, there was a lot of hell that she had to go through. She had to live without her father because her father had to design the railroad tracks for the Germans. Her mother had a little sandwich shop. This was one of the good things that happened in her life.

Because it was such a cold and evil winter, a couple of German Generals came in one day to get something to eat. They saw my mother and asked my grandmother, "May I pick her up?" They were a little bit worried because he was a German soldier and all, but they let him pick her up. The German General gave my grandmother a great great compliment. He said, "From a beautiful woman came a beautiful child."

That evil winter was cold as hell. The next day about three or four German soldier trucks pulled up to my grandmother's sandwich shop and gifts poured out. There was whole bunch of coal to keep the furnace hot for my mother and my grandmother. There were baby clothes by the dozens. There was also baby food and clothes even to keep even my grandmother warm.

All this was because of my mother. It was because of her being such a beautiful baby which captured that German General's heart. At this time, my mother was living in her grandmother's home. It was her mother's mother. My mother did not tell me where her father's parents were or even if they were alive in that period of time. But two years later, they were blessed with a new addition to their family, Janeck Sudomir.

I believe that's how his name is spelled, but it's pronounced by saying the j as the letter y. My mother became the little mama in the family. But one time, the Germans were searching all the residences to see if anybody was harboring any Russians. They came to where my mother was living to search for any Russians and also for another purpose. They came to show the whole town what would happen to anyone who would be harboring any Russians.

The Germans trashed my great grandmother's home. One German soldier knocked over and broke my mother's favorite cup. At four years old, my mother had a favorite cup because it was yellow and to her it was just beautiful. It had all kinds of colors. When the German soldiers were leaving, my mother, at four years old, grabbed that German by the pant leg and told that German off.

She said, "You broke my favorite cup. That was my favorite cup." And because of my mother's bravery, he came back the next day with a very beautiful cup that had a rose on it. He apologized and said, "I hope this can replace your cup. I'm very sorry for knocking it over." But like I was saying the day before, they gathered everyone in the town square, and showed everybody what would happen to anybody harboring any Russians along with any Polish family.

So they were saying, "We will not only kill the Russians, but you and your family as well." They had a big, huge bon fire, and a whole family that was harboring some Russians got burned alive. Some boy kept coming out with fire all over him, and they kept pushing him back into the fire. My mama was only millimeters away from all this, and they made everyone watch.

If the children tried to turn their heads, the soldiers would make sure that their heads turned around so that they could see. This was done to the whole town. After that, my great grandmother took her daughter and my mama, at four years old, to go live with my grandmother's sister. Her name was Hella.

One time it seemed that the Russians wanted to get back at the Germans and so they started hunting German families. Then somebody ratted on my grandmother's aunt's house by saying, "A German family lived there." Who knows why? Maybe they were German themselves." The Russians had taken my mother's cousins, her aunt, I believe my grandmother, and my great grandmother and put them all in the line of fire.

I have a great aunt who was trying to visit the family. I believe it was my grandfather's sister, and her name, coincidently, was Hella. They had put a rifle right into my uncle's face at two years old. My mama, at four years old, smacked that rifle right out of that Russian's arm.

Then the Russian had put the rifle right in my mama's face. My great aunt luckily she spoke Russian as well as Polish. She ran up to these

Russian Generals and explained that they were not German. They were Polish and their neighbors as well were Polish. They were not Germans. The Russians could not tell the Polish people from the German people.

And the Germans, it was the same with them. It was a vicious slaughter era, because as you can see, if my great aunt hadn't arrived at that moment, my mama and her family would have been slaughtered. So the Polish people were making it really hard for the Russians and the Germans to tell each other apart one from another. If they did find one another, they would be tossing them on fences or barbecuing their bodies alive.

The Germans and the Russians did this all for fun to each other. It would be like this one movie I saw called The Great Hunt. Only in The Great Hunt, they would be hunting real vicious animals, and that's just how the Germans and the Russians thought of each other as if both of their people were vicious animals.

My grandfather who worked for the Germans once had a leave of absence, and he brought my mother a little dress. My mother started dancing around outside and saying in Polish, "Oh my God, what a beautiful dress. Mother of God, it is so beautiful. My mother kept dancing around.

She thanked her father so much. My grandfather also had a way of teaching people by example. In other words, punishment. My mother could not go to school at six years old because she had to take care of her four year old brother. She had to wash him, give him baths, do the laundry, and make the dinner for her father and her mother.

One time my mother had stepped in some mud with her shoes that happened to be her dress shoes. So she tried to get the mud off with a cloth. Her father came up to her and asked, "Are you cleaning your shoes?" My mother said yes, "I stepped in some mud." He asked, "Is this the way that you clean your shoes with a cloth from your dress."

She said, "I have nothing else. Let me see your hands. He held her hand out and smacked her hands very hard. He said, "Get in the house, get some shoe polish, wash your shoes, wash your feet, wash the floor, do the laundry, wash your dress and polish those shoes."

In America, children always think that they have it good, and they can talk trash to their parents. Some children who grew up thinking that they a hard life with punishment don't know that they actually had it good. There's no stupid CPS over in Europe. If you so much as do the tinniest thing that your parents would consider wrong, believe me, you will not get the kind of punishment that you think is hell.

You think you will get yelled at. You think you will get the belt. You think you will get soap on your tongue. You think your grounding is bad or the taking of the keys is bad? Try and take this punishment out. If you do anything at seven or eight years old, your punishment will be taking care of the whole house and making dinner. If you have any siblings, you will have to change their diapers also, and all this is whether you're a boy or a girl.

You also get whipped along your back as well as your butt. So all people out here you should try to respect your parents, and thank God you're not living in Europe.

THE BAILEY AND GRAM FAMILY

THE BAILEY AND GRAM FAMILY are two special families to me. You see, they're relatives of the love of my life, Jade. Just about every family event that they have, I am very welcome to. Jade's mother to me is a very special woman. She looks amazingly young.

Her grandchildren always call her Honey. That was a nickname that came from her first grandchild, Kyle and somehow carried on. Kyle is Jade's son. Jade's brothers', Henry, Joshua, and Tom are amazingly kind to me. They are like the brothers I only wish I had. Their kids are extremely intelligent. They look at me almost like an uncle already.

Their wives and my Jade are awesome cooks, and Jades mother doesn't think she can cook at all. Sometimes when I talk with them, we exchange recipes. Henry's daughter, Rose, reads books fast, and she is very intelligent. I sometimes give her some titles of books to read, and sometimes she says, "I already read it." Rose and I have great conversations about books. Violet is Henry's other daughter, and she happens to read too. However, she's a little shy and quiet.

Their son, Bruce is intelligent also. He's headed on to this one company called Bowing on an internship program. He's about sixteen or seventeen, but that's just a guess. I always have conversations with Henry. He's like a friend also. Cindy is Henry's wife. I always find myself in a great conversation with her. She's like a sister that I never had but not to say that the other wives aren't.

Tom has a great family also. His wife's name is Carol. Both of them have three kids. They have two boys and a girl. They are kids that I would be proud to have also. Carol is a great wife and mother. She home schools the kids. When they go somewhere, they do things as a family so they're all very close. I think that's a real blessing. It's something that I wish I had growing up with my family.

Joshua is a great guy and brother. He worries about my Jade just like I do, and he's a great father and husband. Joshua and Candy have five kids. They have four boys and one very special girl. Two of the boys happen to be twins. The other two boys are already altar boys. Their names are Jordan and Tyler. The twins names are Samby and Brandon. They love their little sister. Their little sister who is a year old always runs up to her brothers and gives them hugs and kisses, and the boys do the same. Her name is Sierra.

She's got mama and dada down. She calls Jordan Eh Eh and Tyler Aya. She calls Samby Bra Bra and Brandon Dot-Dot. She has nicknames for Jade and I. She calls me Ju Ju or Juli Ju for Joseph. Sierra is getting very close to my name. Sierra calls Jade Saya and her grandmother as Haya.

Jade's Aunt Rachel and Uncle Brian are very good people as well. They have four kids. Their names are Anthony, Alisa, James and Chase. They treat me like another cousin or like a brother. Anthony and James they already have a little family going. James has a beautiful little girl, and Anthony's son is named Hunter. They're both great and charming little kids.

Rachel and Brian are so proud of their grandchildren. They always like to play with them. The whole family is just a joy to be with. When I'm with Jade and her family, I feel as if I'm already a part of the family which to me is a true blessing. I go to church when I can on Saturdays with Joshua's family, Jade's mother, and the love of my life, Jade. We have a great time.

There was recently a fiesta over there at church. It rained but still we all managed to have a good time. I danced with my beautiful Jade, and while we were dancing, I started singing to her which brought some tears to her eyes. I had a great time with her brother Joshua and his kids, Jade and her mother was a darling to be with. They're all like a family. I wish I could be with all the time.

THE NEGATIVE POSSIBILITIES

RECENTLY, JADE AND I MET a woman one night, and she was very kind. This woman said, "We were definitely meant to be together by the way e looked together. But in order to stay together, everybody in the world including us, should always forget about the past. The past can truly come back to haunt us and destroy us. So now Jade and I are trying to look towards the future.

No one knows what the future will hold, but she said that the way that we look at each other we are definitely twin soulmates. Now here's where it gets a little creepy. The next day I recently had just a small talk with my mother, and she said, "Tonight I need to speak with you and your brother Greg."

I asked what it was about, and she said "It's about me." So I confronted her, and I demanded her to tell me if she was dying. My mama said, "I'm not dying yet. My doctor called earlier and said that I need to get stress out of my life, and maybe you can help me finish my book." I said, "Mama, how about Jade and I help you finish your book. I don't know how to type, but Jade does."

My mother then said, "Not yet. I still need to go a long way in my story." So I told her that the tape recorder that I loaned to you is not working because it's getting background noises. I gave my mama a journal. It was one of my best journals. I said, "Mama, write down whatever you need to say. Cross out anything you don't want to say. This way you don't get no background noises."

My mother said, "Well, then I'm going to have to write in Polish." I said, "That's fine. Write in Polish. When you want us to type it out, you just translate." My mother said, "Thanks, and I love you. I'll try and work on it."

I then met with Jade to work on my book. We started to work on my book right away, but my mind was very stressed out. I started thinking Greg is stressing my mom out very bad, and Victoria and Henry need to be there tonight. I need to try and get a hold of Victoria by leaving her a message by voice and by text message. Victoria never responded. It shows just how much I can't count on Victoria because I wanted her to be there tonight. You see, Victoria needs to see just how much Greg is stressing our mama out.

I went to my mother's tonight, and Greg never showed up. I asked, "Did he call?" My mother said, No not yet." He showed up earlier and just took off again. I ended up helping my mom around the house by doing everything she asked me to do. Anything that she had asked me I always responded yes, Mother. You see, I want to show my mom some respect. I do not want to kill her, but so many people think that I want our mother to die and would do anything to kill her.

Now from what Greg is doing to our mother, she is going to die. Yesterday I got a hold of my Uncle Daniel. About a year before my father died, Uncle Daniel said, "If anyone should try and hurt your mother and you cannot handle it yourself, you get a hold of your uncles Teddy, Tony, and Daniel. We will always help you."

I see you as the strongest one, however, if someone is stressing your mom out or hurting your mom in any way, get a hold of your uncles. They're the heads of the Calkowski family. Otherwise if you don't, you're just letting your mother die. I told my Uncle Charles yesterday in a message what Greg has been doing. I told him how he has been using very foul language towards our mother and raising his voice towards our mother.

I've been trying to help without fighting my brother again so I've been trying to get a hold of our sister Victoria. All she's been doing is just saying, "Why don't you just leave Greg alone. He has enough trouble finding work and working." Victoria needs a serious wake up call because she does not know what hell Greg has been doing.

It's just like she's defending a criminal that has lied to his own attorney. She responded last night to my surprise, but she was too busy to come out because she was working. Today Greg did not come out at all. My mother has been crying all day long and has been needing help with work.

I was helping her ever since I got up. She asked me, "What can we do about this little red neck?" I said then "If Victoria doesn't do anything about this, I'm going to have to go to a family member above her. And she said, "Who's that?" And I yelled, "Uncle Daniel. He'll take care of Greg's ass real good. He's never let you down before. He cares about you a lot and has been a very good brother-in-law for just about 50 years."

She got on the phone, and then I heard in the backyard that my mother talking to Victoria. Of course, Victoria was feeding our mother the same garbage. She was telling our mother that we should just leave Greg alone. Greg is trying to work hard. He has to find hard jobs here and there when she doesn't really know what the heck Greg is really doing.

In Victoria's eyes, Greg is a perfect angel when there's actually a little demon inside him. I tried to yell at my sister while she was still on the phone, but my mother disconnected us just before I could say anything. My mother hung up on purpose so her blood pressure would not go up anymore. My mother's blood pressure is already pushing 220 from having to deal with Greg's garbage and the stress he gives her.

Greg comes and goes and is hardly at home to help our mother. He says he does a lot for this house when he actually leaves the responsibility of his chickens as well as his cats to our mother or myself. They need to be fed. They need to be taken care of, and all he does is come and go. He spends the money on other things that he should be using to take care of his cats and chickens as well as the house and bills. He usually spends it on taxes and beer, concerts, and friends.

Victoria believes it's the other way around. He believes that I do not help at all because I have seizures. He thinks that I just splurge my money from SSI on my girlfriend and myself. I buy our mother food, and today I'm buying her personal products when I shouldn't even have to. Elvis heard me yelling at Victoria in the backyard and thought I was yelling at my mother.

So when I asked him for a ride he said, "You better take care of your mother and not fight with her so much." I swear, I nearly cried because I've been taking care of my mother so much. And today, right after I had tried to yell at Victoria in the backyard, I had said to my mother, "That's it. I'm calling Uncle Daniel."

So I called up my Uncle Daniel again and had to leave another message. I said in the message this time, "I know you care about my mom. If anybody can help my mom, I know it's you Uncle Daniel. You never let my mom down before. I know you would never let her down now. Please get back to me. Don't call my mom because she would probably just deny everything."

But if Greg keeps doing what he's doing, our mom is going to die, Uncle Daniel. My mom and I need your help. So my mom asked me, "What did your Uncle Daniel say?" I told her all I got was his cell phone answering service. She said, "Don't call him again." I said, "Yesterday, I called him and told him about the time that Greg cursed you and me out. And I told him all the horrible words and language that he used against you, and how he treats you like trash." I said to my mother, "Don't worry. "If I know Uncle Daniel, and if he cannot come out or call, he'll pass on the word and someone else will take care of Greg's rear." Uncle Daniel may be eighty five years old, but he'll take care of Greg.

My mother said, "Well, what if he can't come out?" I said, "He'll probably call Greg and give him one heck of a talking to or he can probably send out cousin Greg." My mother said, "Do you know that you could probably start a family war?" I said, "That Greg has already started one."

My mom called me just a little while after I left to meet beautiful future wife, Jade. My mother asked me if my Uncle Daniel had called me yet. I said, "Not yet, but Greg's friend Mike had called me and was sticking behind Greg all the way." He was saying things like, "Are you helping out in any way?" I had already told him for two days now that I had been helping her out.

My mother is trying to do Greg's work as well, and he needs to get his butt here. I told him our mother's blood pressure is pushing 220. Also, if we don't get his help, our mother will die. He just keeps hanging around with you guys. Mike just said, "Well, I'll try and get a hold of him." Mike doesn't give a crap about my mom. He only cares about keeping his grandmother alive.

Greg helps him because Greg gets paid to help his grandmother out. Greg doesn't give a damn about his own mother. I could tell you this, if our mother dies, Greg will be kicked out of the family. I will do it personally.

THE PRESENT THE FUTURE

TODAY THINGS ARE LOOKING PRETTY bad because of personal issues that happened with Jade and her mother as well. Things with Jade and I are going great. I have no complaints there. We ran into a woman that we met the other day. She calls us twin soulmates and says that we just have to keep on moving into the future and forget about the evil past because the past will haunt us.

Also that if we start talking about the past, it will lead to arguing about it. It will also destroy us. So both Jade and myself are trying very hard to just move ahead and forget about everything that was behind us. This is another reason why I'm writing this book. It's like my journal. All the bad stuff is just getting out.

However, I just want people to know what I have gone through in life. I would like people to think to themselves that this guy had it hard, but he still kept on going. Other people that may have had worse situations or even a harder kind of life, can learn from my experience to just keep on going and put the past behind them.

I am one of the last of my kin. My family is nearly all gone. Luckily, my older brother had a son. But other than my nephew, if my younger brother and I should end up passing without any Aires, our family is through.

By this book and others to come, I am leaving behind my legacy of how I grew, how I lived, and what I lived for. I hope that through all my books people everywhere can learn a little bit of how to not take life for granite and to live every day such as if it would be your last.

Also, I finally got my head screwed on straight and woke up and smelled the coffee. I finally married Jade and should consider myself very lucky after what he put her through.

We also started having amazing adventures together. But that's another story.

Dr. Joseph C. Calkowski

Printed in the United States
By Bookmasters